# Cyrus Vance

# The American Secretaries of State and Their Diplomacy

ROBERT H. FERRELL, Editor

## VOLUME XX

# Cyrus Vance

DAVID S. McLELLAN

ROWMAN & ALLANHELD
PUBLISHERS

ROWMAN & ALLANHELD

Published in the United States of America in 1985
by Rowman & Allanheld, Publishers
(a division of Littlefield, Adams & Company)
81 Adams Drive, Totowa, New Jersey 07512

Copyright © 1985 by Rowman & Allanheld

**Library of Congress Cataloging in Publication Data**

McLellan, David S.
  Cyrus Vance.

  (The American secretaries of states and their
diplomacy ; v. 20)
  Bibliography: p.
  Includes index.
  1. Vance, Cyrus R. (Cyrus Roberts), 1917–
2. Statesmen—United States—Biography. 3. Cabinet
officers—United States—Biography. 4. United States—
Foreign relations—1977–1981. I. Title. II. Series.
E183.7.B462   vol. 20     973 s      85-10785
[E840.8.V36]      [973.926′092′4]   [B]
ISBN 0-8476-7146-1

85  86  87  /  10  9  8  7  6  5  4  3  2  1
Printed in the United States of America

*To*
Brenda Handforth Kome
*in*
*loving memory*

# Contents

# Acknowledgments

I wish to express my appreciation to the Woodrow Wilson Center of the Smithsonian Institution in Washington for appointment as a visiting fellow for the autumn of 1983, a position which made possible the completion of research and interviews for this book. The many kindnesses extended by the staff and by the director, James Billington, were indispensable.

I also wish to acknowledge Miami University for providing a sabbatical leave during the winter quarter of 1984 to help complete the writing.

The Reverend Richard W. Schell, headmaster of the Kent School, was especially helpful in describing Secretary Vance's preparatory school years. Several colleagues at the Wilson Center carefully discussed my work, among them Shlomo Avineri, General William Young Smith, and Robert Jaster. I would also like to thank my Miami University colleagues—Dan Jacobs, William Jackson, Will Hazelton, William Campbell, and Reo Christiansen, as well as Robert Tucker of Princeton University. Donald Oehlerts, director of the King Library, and his staff and Eileen Wiley, supervisor of the university mailroom, helped lighten my tasks.

I owe Jean West and Betty Marak a debt of gratitude for typing and retyping. Finally I would like to thank my wife, Ann Handforth McLellan, for assistance in every aspect of the pages that follow.

# CHAPTER ONE

# *Years of Preparation*

Cyrus Vance was born in Clarksburg, West Virginia, on March 27, 1917, the second son of John and Amy Roberts Vance. His father was of an established West Virginia family, his mother from Philadelphia. In 1918 the family moved to Bronxville, New York, from whence Vance's father could commute to Manhattan as an insurance executive. Some years later, in 1922, the elder Vance died suddenly of pneumonia. The bereaved family spent a year in Switzerland, where the two boys, Cyrus and his older brother, John, lived with a Swiss family and attended the Institut Sillig, a private school in Vevey. There the boys learned French. The task of raising the two sons meanwhile had fallen to their mother, a thoughtful woman of character who would inculcate a sense of moral values.

From young Cyrus's early years it was fairly clear that the youth might become a lawyer. His uncle was John W. Davis, the eminent lawyer and Democratic candidate for President in 1924.[1] Uncle John had no sons, and Vance remembered going to his house on Sunday mornings and being interrogated on leading cases of the day. Davis provided a window to the world of law and politics. Upon resignation as Ambassador to the Court of St. James in 1921, he had become head of the Wall Street firm of Davis, Polk and Wardwell. In 1922 he was elected president of the American Bar Association. His reputation was achieved as an appellate lawyer—he argued more cases (141) before the Supreme Court than any lawyer of his time. "Of all the persons who appeared before the Court in my time," wrote Justice Oliver Wendell Holmes, Jr., "there was never anybody more elegant, more concise or more logical than John W. Davis." An economic and social conservative, Davis did much of his legal work for big corporations. But he was also a civil libertarian until late in his career when he argued for the State of South Carolina in favor of the "separate but equal" doctrine in the case of *Brown v. Board of Education*.

Vance in 1930 followed his brother to the Kent School in Connecticut, an Episcopal institution that stood for Christian devotion and idealism.[2] Kent had an enduring influence on his character. At Kent he acquired not only an education but an apprenticeship in responsibility. The headmaster and founder, Father Frederick Sill, intended the school to be run by the students, even to the point of taking responsibility for disciplining their peers. Vance was one of three senior prefects chosen by classmates to run the student government.

It was at Kent that Vance began to develop into a young man of promise. At Kent he was an outstanding athlete, winning letters in football, becoming captain of the hockey team and a member of the 1934 crew that made the Henley Regatta. The coach tagged him "a perfect sport and a gentleman," a phrase that in his later years as Secretary of State may have become wearisome. He graduated from Kent in May 1935, and that fall entered Yale, an economics major and classmate of William Scranton, William Bundy, Stanley Resor, and others who years afterward gained prominence in the Kennedy administration. Among his classmates was the lawyer and author Louis Auchincloss, whose novels about the practice of law in the great New York firms would mirror the careers of Vance and his classmates.[3] At Yale, Vance took his studies seriously and was able to combine academic achievement with an active social life and participation in athletics. He was "tapped" for Scroll and Key and elected to the Torch Honor Society. He also joined the Fence Club and became a member of the hockey team.

Summers between college years he worked with a half-dozen other Yale students at the Grenfell mission on the Northwest River in Labrador. Wilfred T. Grenfell, the exponent of "muscular Christianity," had visited Labrador in 1892 as a medical missionary, and was so shocked by what he later described as "the poverty and ignorance and semi-starvation" of the people—English, Indian,

Eskimo alike—that he determined to devote his life to their better-ment. For the next forty years he raised money to establish hospitals, schools, and craft centers whose good work attracted volunteers like Vance and his fellow students. Vance was never to lose sight of the importance of voluntary aid. A half-century later, as president of the New York Bar Association, he made a stubborn but not too successful effort to persuade the lawyers of New York City to devote Saturdays to providing the needy of New York with free legal advice.

In Yale Law School, Vance made his mark, obtaining an LL.B. with honors in 1942. After receiving his degree, he enlisted immediately in the U.S. Navy under the officer training program. He saw duty as a gunnery officer aboard destroyers at Bougainville, Tarawa, Saipan, Guam, and the Philippines, and was discharged in March 1946 with the rank of lieutenant, senior grade.

The future Secretary of State met Gay Sloane while at Yale. Gay was studying at the Parsons School of Design. They became engaged while Vance was in midshipman's school, but waited until after the war to be married. Gay's family were founders of the W. and J. Sloane Company of New York City.

After the war Vance passed the New York State bar examination and joined the Wall Street firm of Simpson, Thatcher and Bartlett. He and the firm were well matched. More in the 1940s perhaps than today, Wall Street was looking for young men from socially connected families who would "fit in" as well as possess intellectual credentials. A later sociological study of Wall Street lawyers found that the big firms "prefer the man with all three attributes: lineage, ability, and personality."[4] They wanted lawyers who were "Nordic, have pleasing personalities, are graduates of the 'right' school, have the right social background."[5] Slightly more than half the young lawyers who entered Simpson, Thatcher and Bartlett in 1945 or after (Vance's group) and who had left by a dozen or so years later (after Vance became a partner) departed mainly because they knew they were not going to be partners. According to the same study, in selecting partners, Wall Street firms looked for not only the right social background, but also outstanding ability and enthusiasm for hard work. A partner had to be able to "see all the angles" of a legal problem, be painstakingly careful, have a keen sense of the law and an ability to get along with people—which meant patience and tolerance. He had to be committed to getting the best deal for his clients. Above all the associate who makes partner must demonstrate stamina for work: "ability and 'hard, hard work' are musts for the associate if he expects to become a partner."[6] The associate who hopes to get ahead is indentured for ten years of unremitting intellectual labor, often working into the night and through weekends. His work is usually under direction of a partner whose judgment will determine whether he stays.

The rewards of success in a firm were of two kinds—financial, and a certain joy of achievement. Richard Powell's hero in *The Philadelphian* summed it up: "The way I look at it . . . in a big firm it's a tough climb to the top, but a mighty nice view if you can get there. I don't want to get to the top in a small firm and find I still can't see over the heads of the crowd. I'll take my chances in a big firm."[7]

Vance's law career was not the only source of self-fulfillment during the early years of his marriage. He and Gay shared the postwar commitment to a large family and were soon parents of five children. Marriage, family and membership in the Episcopal Church were to provide a balance and counterpart to the demanding pressures of his law career.

There has been a tendency of late to disparage the lawyer as statesman, but the Wall Street lawyer may receive better preparation for conducting foreign policy than he is given credit for. The corporate lawyer is a researcher, writer, and reviser of briefs; he confers with partners, associates, and clients; directs a staff or team; revises corporate charters and by-laws; prepares trial memos and engages in corporate work and banking matters both domestic and foreign. This type of experience was to be very useful to Vance in his role as Secretary of State.

For ten years—1947 to 1957—Vance immersed himself in civil litigation and procedure. Much of his work was as a trial lawyer handling a large range of cases. Vance's liberalism strengthened during those years. The Wall Street lawyer is not likely to experience at first hand the hardships of the poor, but he is likely to acquire an appreciation of government regulation and welfare socialism as buffers against economic disorder. As a lifelong Democrat, and conscious of the privileges of wealth, Vance deepened his commitment to the idea of social responsibility during this period. His interests, which became concentrated in the area of international affairs, found expression with his membership in the Council on Foreign Relations.

The Council on Foreign Relations had its genesis in the dissatisfaction felt by some internationally minded Americans with the outcome of the Paris Peace Conference of 1919. It was established to provide high-ranking officers of banking, manufacturing, and the legal profession in the New York area with an outlet for discussing and influencing the direction of U.S. foreign policy through meetings and participation in study groups drawn from the universities and the world of professional diplomacy. Its prestige and the reknown of its journal, *Foreign Affairs*, made it the launching ground for the careers of many eminent American statesmen, including John Foster Dulles and Henry Kissinger.

Simpson, Thatcher and Bartlett encouraged both associates and partners to participate in politics,[8] and almost as soon as he had become a partner, Vance responded to the call to Washington. It was about that time that the Soviet Union fired off Sputnik (October 1957), producing emotional shock waves throughout the United States. Americans had taken for granted that the United States had an unbeatable lead in military technology. For the Russians to launch a missile into space was felt to be a severe blow.

Panic prompted government initiatives to recapture America's lead (or, in President Dwight D. Eisenhower's mind, to demonstrate that we had not lost it). The President appointed a blue-ribbon panel chaired by a San Francisco lawyer, H. Rowland Gaither, to inquire into America's defenses. Not to be outdone, Senator Lyndon B. Johnson, the majority leader and candidate for the Democratic nomination for President, initiated his own probe. The Senate resolution establishing a thirteen-member committee to make recommendations on the United States's space program was introduced February 5, 1958, and adopted next day by a 78 to 1 roll call. It provided for a committee of seven Democrats and six Republicans, with Johnson as chairman. The group was charged with reporting to the Senate "by bill or otherwise," by June 1, 1958, a plan for supervision of space efforts. In introducing the resolution, Johnson argued the need to settle the question of whether the military or a civil agency should have "specific responsibility for America's effort in outer space."

Senator Johnson recruited Edward Weisl, one of Vance's senior law partners, and Weisl asked Vance to go to Washington with him as special counsel to the Preparedness Investigation Committee.[9] Vance worked with the committee, taking testimony and preparing a report calling for an independent civil agency—the National Aeronautics and Space Agency. NASA was not to supplant the Pentagon in weapons and missile development, but keep the military from getting control of the space program. The bill establishing the new agency was reported out on June 11. As for the investigation itself, Vance and his group had concluded that there was a "missile gap" between the U.S. and the U.S.S.R. but that it was not nearly as serious as the one projected by alarmists. Belief in the existence of a missile gap was mainly the result of inadequate information, as well as the deliberate scare tactics of the Soviets.

The experience was a valuable one for Vance, who was able to establish his effectiveness and broaden his connections. When John F. Kennedy was elected to the presidency in 1960 it was not surprising that Vance, with ties to the President-elect's friend McGeorge Bundy and brother-in-law Sargent Shriver, would be appointed general counsel of the Department of Defense.

Upon entering the Pentagon in January 1961, Vance soon received a difficult assignment, dealing with the Cubans following the disastrous Bay of Pigs invasion. How was he to obtain release of the prisoners of Premier Fidel Castro, and how deal with the Cuban community in America? The solution was a ransom consisting of millions of dollars worth of medicines and tractors. The Cuban community, however, remained unhappy.

A second Pentagon assignment came from Secretary of Defense Robert S. McNamara, who, as part of a plan for reorganizing the Department of Defense and strengthening the authority of the secretary, established an Office of Management Planning and Organization Studies and put Vance in charge. This office was to determine how to run the department more effectively and at the same time give the secretary closer control over what was going on. Despite the Defense Reorganization Act of 1947, the Pentagon was still a collection of service fiefdoms, each developing its missions and weapons. Vance's charge was to remedy such ills as well as to improve logistics and strategic planning. Although McNamara's reforms were bound to arouse resentment, Vance's handling of the reorganization and reforms was expert.[10] While McNamara took public heat, Vance moved the department in the right direction.

When Elvis J. Stahr, Jr., resigned as Secretary of the Army in June 1962 to become president of Indiana University, Vance replaced him. Washington was now hearing complaints that McNamara and his administrative "whiz kids" under Charles Hitch were trespassing on terrain that belonged to the military. Stahr left with a parting blast, asserting that command in the Pentagon was becoming overcentralized. Vance did not share this view. He endeavored to alleviate the Army's concern by listening to their point of view, and representing them to McNamara. In fact the Kennedy administration was spending a great deal more on defense than had Eisenhower, and the Army was enjoying an expansion.

When Roswell Gilpatrick in 1964 resigned as Deputy Secretary of Defense, Vance replaced him. In the wake of Kennedy's assassination, and before Kennedy's successor, President Johnson, escalated the U.S. role in Vietnam, the appointment passed almost unnoticed. Although Secretary of the Army and then Deputy Secretary of Defense, Vance did not find himself in the inner circle of administration officials who made the decisions that took the country into the Vietnam War. By his own testimony he was occasionally present at meetings of the principals, and he has recalled that decisions were taken only after deliberations in which the President participated in the give-and-take, and that decisions appeared to reflect the advice Johnson received.[11] Therein, of course, lay a problem.

The American foreign policy process is dominated by the President. Bureaucratic struggles may take place, but large issues such as war and peace are decided within bounds set by the President—which in Johnson's case meant a combination, as one observer remarked, of "an enormous inferiority complex in regard to handling affairs of state, and an enormous feeling of superiority . . . and self-confidence in handling and manipulating . . . American politics."[12] The result was that the President's advisers, with the exception of Undersecretary of State George Ball, were so carried away by the imperatives of American power and responsibility that none had the judgment to question the course of action.[13] None, including Vance, appears to have had any doubt about the decisions. This was the impression Vance later gave of his own thinking, although Vance did warn McNamara in a July 1965 memo that the "overall cost of mobilizing the forces needed to support a 100,000 man army in Vietnam is likely to be on the order of $8 billion in the coming year," not the several hundred million being talked about.[14] Only after the war had been going for about a year did he begin to sense that the promised result of American military involvement was not to be realized, but like McNamara he chose to suppress his doubts and proceed as if something acceptable might still come out of the war—a stalemate if nothing else. This illusion was maintained, however, at a steadily escalating cost. Townsend Hoopes, in his post as Deputy Secretary of Defense for international security affairs, later wrote of the "ever lengthening shadow that the war was casting over U.S. relations in every other part of the world, including the home front."[15]

Early in the war a dividing line was laid down that separated Vance, like McNamara, from the professional military men: the air campaign against North Vietnam. Partly out of concern not to draw the Communist powers into the war, partly out of humanity as well as a growing sense of the ineffectiveness of such an attack against so determined a foe, Vance and McNamara stood against expanding the air war in the way that the military claimed was needed to bring Hanoi to its knees.[16] The enemy was proving far tougher than McNamara and Vance had been led to expect; there was much reason to believe that attempting to bomb North Vietnam "back into the stone age" would not end the war.

By the spring of 1967, Vance and McNamara shared increasing disenchantment with the war and the catastrophic loss of proportion to which it had given rise. Just as McNamara, however, chose not to break with the President and come out publicly in favor of a negotiated end to the war, so Vance maintained loyalty to McNamara. McNamara might "argue the case for moderation with the President—privately, selectively, intermittently."[17] The unspoken corollary seemed to be that no issue or difference with President Johnson was sufficient to require resignation. From what Vance later said, it would appear that he and other second-echelon officials were quite aware of the magnitude of the catastrophe, but could not impress their views on the President. Speaking of the March 1968 briefings by elder statesmen—including former Secretary of State Dean Acheson—to whom Johnson turned for advice, briefings that led to the President's decision to ask for a cease-fire, Vance afterward stated that he heard nothing in the course of those briefings that he had not already heard within the government.[18]

Meanwhile, beset by a back ailment that forced him to work lying down most of the day, Vance finally submitted his resignation in June 1967. He returned to his law firm, but continued an active involvement in public affairs. Not only did he take on troubleshooting for President Johnson, but was elected president of the New York Bar Association and a fellow of the Yale Corporation. He wrote a pamphlet espousing arms control for the American Association for the United Nations. He supported Sargent Shriver and Senator Edmund Muskie in their unsuccessful bids for the Democratic presidential nomination in 1968. In such ways the years passed, and Vance slowly moved toward the front rank of individuals who would be considered for appointment to high government office.

CHAPTER TWO

# Crisis Manager

In the course of duties in the Pentagon, both in the Department of the Army and in the Department of Defense, Vance encountered several opportunities to act as a negotiator, on matters domestic and' foreign. Here were experiences necessary for a future Secretary of State. The first concerned the Panama Canal Zone, where in January 1963, after years of contention, the local residents—the "Zonians"—and the Panamanian government had agreed to fly United States and Panamanian flags side by side in recognition of Panama's titular sovereignty over the zone. In January 1965, American high school students in the zone, urged on by their parents, attempted again to fly only the American flag. Mobs invaded the zone in protest, six Panamanians were killed, hundreds more were wounded, rioting spread throughout Panama, and portions of the zone came under attack from snipers.

To get control in the Canal Zone, President Johnson dispatched Secretary of the Army Vance and Undersecretary of State Thomas Mann.[1] Vance's job was to see that every effort was being made to minimize the violence while Mann negotiated. Meanwhile the United States persuaded a meeting of the Organization of American States on January 11 to appoint a commission, which arrived on the scene the next day. After talks between Mann, Vance, the commission, and Panamanian authorities, an agreement was reached to withdraw U.S. forces from the border in return for the Panamanian national guard's clearing of their side of snipers and troublemakers. Although the United States rejected the idea that it should renegotiate its lease of the Canal Zone, here was the beginning of a long process of returning sovereignty to the Panamanians, a process that Vance would conclude twelve years later.

The second of Vance's negotiations, which took place in late April 1965, involved the Dominican Republic. Following the assassination in 1961 of dictator Rafael Trujillo, who had ruled the republic for thirty years, the Kennedy administration had supported the election of a noncommunist but left-leaning figure, Dr. Juan Bosch, as president. Bosch had scarcely begun to grapple with Trujillo's legacy before he was overthrown by a coup in September 1963. The successor regime, led by Donald Reid Cabral, was beset by economic troubles and rivalries within the military. A group of younger officers launched a coup on April 24, 1965, calling for return of Bosch, then living in Puerto Rico. A countermovement took form under Brigadier General Wessin y Wessin, responsible for the overthrow of Bosch, and it gained the support of a panicky American ambassador and the State Department's hardline anti-leftist Latin American specialist, Undersecretary Mann.

Disturbed by reports from the embassy and from former Ambassador John Bartlow Martin of a possible communist coup, President Johnson authorized an occupation by 20,000 Marines, ostensibly to protect American lives and property but in fact to influence the political outcome. Deployed through the city of Santo Domingo, the Marines positioned themselves between the junta led by Brigadier General Antonio Imbert Barreya and the rebels led by Colonel Francisco Caamaño Deño. The obvious political purpose of American intervention aroused a torrent of protest from Latin American governments, and forced the administration to repair the damage by asking intercession by the Organization of American States. No credence was given to Washington's claim that American lives were in danger.

To promote a new political deal for the Dominican people, while protecting the U.S. stake, the President dispatched a much publicized mission consisting of McGeorge Bundy, Mann, Assistant Secretary of State Jack Hood Vaughn, and Deputy Secretary of Defense Vance. Bundy and Vance stopped off in Puerto Rico to see whether Bosch might form a government acceptable to a majority of the Dominican people. As leader of the Constitutional party and of the movement opposing military rule, Bosch took the position that only appointment of his colleague S. Antonio Guzmán as provisional chief executive would provide the chance to form a government of national reconciliation. Bundy and Vance flew on to the Dominican Republic to attempt to do this. But the mission was divided, Bundy and Vance believing that representatives of Bosch's Constitutional party should be in the new government, with perhaps even Guzmán as provisional president, whereas Mann did not share that view. If a civil war was to be averted, some agreement would have to be worked out. Vance's assignment was to get the local military chiefs to resign and permit appointment of officers acceptable to a new civil leadership. At one point they had all agreed to tender their resignations, only to have General Imbert dissuade them. Much later Vance was told by the Dominican foreign minister that the Imbert junta had discussed the idea of getting rid of Vance by shooting him.[2]

Neither side in the Dominican Republic would accept the U.S. terms. The junta was told it would have to accept Guzmán, pending elections, but Guzmán was told he would have to agree not only to send alleged Communists out of the country, but also several leaders of the Constitutional party, including Colonel Caamaño. It would appear that such were Mann's (and Washington's) conditions for Guzmán, and that Bundy and Vance might have settled for a more limited purge, which Guzmán was in any case unable to deliver. Because Guzmán would not agree to the American terms, the mission failed and fighting continued, although the presence of U.S. Marines did reduce the level of violence. The mission's activity at least provided the OAS with an opportunity to take over the negotiation and work out a compromise.

Having taken part in two crises of foreign policy, Vance found that his next crisis was domestic. He had resigned as Deputy Secretary of Defense in June 1967 and left for a trip to Europe with his wife. His mother died and he had to return. That same weekend came rioting, burning, and looting in the black ghetto of Detroit. This was becoming a pattern as black anger, unleashed by the halting white response to the civil rights movement, exploded in America's cities. Vance returned to Washington from his mother's funeral in Clarksburg, West Virginia, on Sunday evening, and next morning received a call from McNamara asking whether he would be able to go to Detroit and take over direction of federal forces sent to restore order. Despite his continuing back trouble Vance agreed, provided he could take his wife to help him dress and put on and remove his shoes.[3] The situation was complicated because Mayor Cavanagh and Governor Romney were asking for Regular Army troops. The Michigan National Guard was already on the scene but inadequate to the task. Vance arrived at the White House to find that the 82nd Airborne Division at Fort Bragg, under General Throckmorton, was being issued orders. Washington would authorize its use if Romney was prepared to state the need in writing. Arrangements had been going on since 5:00 A.M. The President explained to Vance that he was delegating to him all responsibility and that "I should take such action as I believed necessary."[4] This was a highly anomalous situation. He was being sent as a private citizen to take command of military forces in Detroit. To accompany him he designated Warren Christopher and John Doar from the Attorney General's office, as well as the general counsel of the Army, Alfred B. Fitt, the Deputy Assistant Secretary of Defense for public affairs, Daniel Henkin, and Colonel John Elder.

Vance and his group arrived at Selfridge Air Base outside Detroit and met General Throckmorton, whose forces were en route from Bragg. The rest of the day was spent evaluating the situation with the mayor and Governor Romney, making an inspection of burned-out parts of the city, and meeting with a delegation of black leaders, including Congressmen John Conyers Jr. and Charles Diggs. Conyers was against use of the airborne troops, now arriving twenty-five miles north of Detroit, and Vance was inclined to agree that there was insufficient basis to justify their deployment. But as evening advanced and reports of sniping, looting, and violence picked up, he ordered in the 82nd Airborne.

Vance and his staff remained in Detroit for the next week, while troops restored order. His final report became something of a handbook for authorities in other cities confronting violence. It also led to his recommending to the Kerner Commission (the National Advisory Commission on Civil Disorder) an increase in black and other minority members in the National Guard, and training of the Guard in fire discipline to minimize indiscriminate shooting.

That autumn (of 1967) the president asked Vance to take on another crisis—again diplomatic—this time to mediate the conflict between Greece and Turkey over Cyprus. Although Cyprus had gained independence from Great Britain in the early 1960s, it had remained a focus of conflict.[5] The population consisted of a Greek majority and a Turkish minority. To gain independence from Britain the Greek Cypriots, led by Archbishop Makarios, had to agree to forego *enosis* or union with Greece and to respect the rights of the Turks. Instead, the island was a frequent scene of violent incidents between Greeks and Turks, against which the Turkish government in Ankara raised strong protests. To make matters worse, the Greek government in Athens, always under strong pressure to back Archbishop Makarios, who had become head of the Cypriot government, authorized the stationing of 10,000 Greek army troops on Cyprus in violation of the 1964 independence accords.

Pressure had been mounting in Turkey to challenge Greek violation of agreements governing the island and especially the rights of the Turkish minority. Just when the Turkish government appeared to have determined to make removal of most of the Greek troops an issue with the newly installed military junta in Athens, those troops again (November 15) attacked Turkish enclaves. Public outrage in Turkey brought the Turkish government to the brink of intervention. Turkish forces were readied for an invasion, and on November 18 in an ultimatum to the Greek government (bypassing the wily Makarios), Turkey insisted on removal of Greek troops. These events gave Turkey the chance to reassert its involvement in the island. The military junta in Athens recognized that it was an unpopular regime in an unpopular (and illegal) situation and prepared to yield. Makarios then became intransigent.

If the United States was not to see two North Atlantic Treaty Organization allies at war, action was called for. On November 22, Vance received a call from Undersecretary of State Nicholas Katzenbach informing him that the Turkish government might invade Cyprus next day and asking if he would leave that afternoon. Vance consulted his partners. By 12:15 those he could find (it being the day before Thanksgiving) had agreed that he should go. No sooner had he so informed Katzenbach than he got a call that the department was sending a cable to Athens and Ankara requesting permission for him to come and that a plane would be waiting at Kennedy

Airport no later than 4:00 P.M. Vance called his wife, who was herself packing in anticipation of a trip to Virginia to spend the holiday with one of their daughters. The first his wife knew of what was afoot was when he asked her to pack his bag and meet him at the airport.

Authorization from the Turkish government arrived late, so Vance and his State Department adviser John Walsh and the interpreters did not take off until 6:30. Knowing it was the Turks who intended to invade, Vance decided to find out their terms. He would then talk to the Greek government. Makarios would be left to Manlio Brosio, the permanent secretary of NATO, and to José Rolz-Bennett, a U.N. official, who was also being dispatched to deal with the crisis. The flight was taken up with reading cables from the embassies in Ankara and Athens. The plane flew nonstop, New York to Ankara, landing at daybreak at a fighter strip amidst a late-November fall of snow. The President's instructions were to stop a war.

Vance began what was perhaps a first venture in shuttle diplomacy. He sounded the Turkish government's terms. After two trips between Ankara and Athens he decided it would be impossible to get either country to agree to the other's terms, and he would have to act as mediator. With his aide, Walsh, and the two American ambassadors, he devised a four-point proposal, the gist of which was to remove Greek Army forces from Cyprus and guarantee the safety of the Turkish community.

The Turkish foreign minister was initially favorable, but cabinet and opposition leaders refused to accept the American proposal. After a day of waiting, Vance was called to the foreign ministry, to learn that he would have to negotiate with the cabinet, which was in a room next to that of the foreign minister. The sticking point was a demand that almost all Greek forces be removed within a time that Vance considered unreasonable. He asked to see Prime Minister Suleiman Demeril, and after a difficult session the latter secured the cabinet's agreement to give the Greeks more time to get their troops out. Anxious to avoid a war that could lead to disaster, and to regain U.S. support after their overthrow of civil government in Athens, the junta quickly agreed to Vance's formula. Makarios had been held in check by Brosio and Rolz-Bennett and had little choice but to accept.

The Greek-Turkish crisis gave Vance opportunity to observe

firsthand that some problems of American foreign policy had nothing to do with the Soviet Union but were caused by revolutions, communal rivalries, and regional conflicts in which the U.S. could best play the role of peacemaker.

In early 1968 came another mission—this time caused by interception of the U.S. Navy's electronic spy ship, *Pueblo*, by vessels of the North Korean navy. There had also been an attack, presumably by North Korean terrorists, on the Blue House, the residence of South Korean President Park Chung Hee. This combination of events created a tense atmosphere in Korean circles, and Ambassador William J. Porter cabled that Park might take some unpredictable action, such as an attack on North Korea. Vance flew to Seoul as the President's emissary, to make sure that there was no misunderstanding of American policy. The United States had the Vietnam War on its hands and could not afford to become involved in another armed conflict. Vance was blunt with Park: there must be no military action without consultation, indeed no such action should be taken at all; negotiation to secure release of the crew of the *Pueblo* would be carried on by the U.S. Government with the North Koreans, without the South Koreans' presence. Vance received another lesson, this time in the need for decisiveness in dealing with a less powerful ally contemplating an action detrimental to U.S. interests.

The next assignment followed upon President Johnson's decision of March 31, 1968, to initiate negotiations for a cease-fire with North Vietnam. In making the announcement, the President spoke of no conditions for the simultaneous partial bombing halt he had instituted, and said nothing of circumstances that might require resumption of bombing. The bombing halt was partial because it extended only above the 19th parallel. Between the 19th and 17th parallels the administration intended to continue the bombing to protect the DMZ line and keep the pressure on Hanoi. Three days later the government of North Vietnam offered to begin negotiations. A month passed before agreement on a site—Paris—could be reached. Vance was named deputy chief negotiator under W. Averell Harriman.

In addition to Harriman and Vance, the American team to negotiate with North Vietnam consisted of the gruff, knowledgeable Philip

Habib from the State Department; William Jordan, an ex-newspaperman who had joined the staff of the President's Adviser for National Security; Walt W. Rostow, by way of the State Department; Daniel Davidson, Harriman's special assistant; and General Andrew Goodpaster. It was, in one observer's words, "Small and high powered, able, patient and imaginative."[6]

The terms that Harriman and Vance offered were essentially those set out in the so-called San Antonio formula of the previous autumn, as modified by the new Secretary of Defense, Clark Clifford. According to this formula the United States would stop all bombing of North Vietnam "when this will lead promptly to productive discussions. We would assume that while discussions proceed, North Vietnam would not take advantage of the bombing cessation or limitation."

To the American demand that Hanoi take no advantage, Hanoi countered with a demand that the complete bombing halt be unconditional. By late July 1968, Vance and his co-negotiators had developed a formula to get around the "no advantage" versus "no conditions" stalemate. The United States would stop all bombing and Hanoi would agree to restore and observe the demilitarized buffer zone along the 17th parallel. The Americans would let the North Vietnamese know that any bombing cessation would be on the "assumption" that the North Vietnamese would not attack cities of South Vietnam. The problem Harriman and Vance faced was to get assurances that would satisfy President Johnson, who was under pressure to continue bombing so long as there was no assurance that Hanoi would not renew its offensive in the south. Johnson's initial response to the Harriman-Vance proposal for a simple understanding was negative. According to one observer, Chester Cooper, it touched a raw nerve in the President to be informed that unless progress could be made the Democratic party would be at a disadvantage in that year's presidential election.[7] And of course the North Vietnamese gave no indication that they would be responsive to an American assumption, such as Vance proposed, that would enable the bombing to halt and the conference to open.

Before negotiation could begin, it was necessary to be sure of its basis, and the President rebuffed a proposal from Paris that a lull in the fighting that summer might be treated as an assumption that

Hanoi was ready to move toward peace, and "an important opportunity for peace as seen by Harriman and Vance slipped away."[8] In an address to the Veterans of Foreign Wars on August 19, Johnson declared that the United States would not stop the bombing "until it had reason to believe that the other side intends seriously to join with us in de-escalating the war and moving seriously toward peace."

The other obstacle to negotiation proved to be opposition by the government in Saigon to negotiating with the National Liberation Front. Here again Vance and his associates figured a way out.

> The idea was simply to refer to "two sides," leaving it to each "side" to work out its own composition. Thus if the Hanoi delegation wished to regard the National Liberation Front as a separate body it could do so. Thus was fashioned the "our side-your side formula."[9]

These contentions remained throughout August and September. In a meeting with Johnson in early October, Vance persuaded the President that

> there really was a chance of a breakthrough and asked for further authority which would permit us to make certain assumptions; and to make it clear to the North Vietnamese what those assumptions were and what action we expected them to take; and further that they would understand what the consequences might be if they did not act in accordance with our stated assumptions. We said we thought that if this could be done that we could get ourselves around the semantic problem of reciprocity (their demand for an unconditional cessation of the bombing vs. the American demand that no military advantage would be taken of such a bombing halt) . . .[10]

Johnson agreed to give it a try, and Vance and Secretary of State Dean Rusk worked out the language of American assumptions and the action expected of North Vietnam if bombing was not to resume. "It was indeed that formula which was used and which finally brought about the agreement (on the part of Hanoi) and the cessation of the bombing."[11] On October 31, 1968, Johnson announced that all bombing and shelling of North Vietnam would stop as of 8:00 A.M., Washington time, November 1.

When it was announced that the conference would meet on November 6, South Vietnam bowed out, refusing to sit with representatives of the National Liberation Front. State Department officials felt that the South Vietnamese had never understood the our side–your side formula. Vance, however, believed that Saigon all along had understood that the intention was a conference at which they and the National Liberation Front would participate. "In my mind," Vance recalled, "this was one of the great tragedies in history; that the South Vietnamese doublecrossed the United States, which I clearly feel they did."[12] Weeks thereafter were wasted haggling over the shape of the table that would permit the National Liberation Front to be seated without giving it the status Saigon wished to deny it, and it was not until November 27 that Saigon at last agreed. Getting Saigon to participate was the first time in this conflict that Washington "exerted the kind of leverage [vis-à-vis its less powerful ally] that its relative strength and national interests warranted."[13] By then it was too late, and a Republican negotiating team headed by Henry Cabot Lodge, Jr., prepared to take over.

Can we say that Vance learned something from this Paris experience in 1967? Having already seen how easy it was to get into a war, now he saw at firsthand what made it so hard to get out: other states—friends and enemies—often were beyond America's power to control. Having their own needs and priorities, they did not hesitate to place their own interests above those of their ally. After leaving Paris, Vance watched the Nixon administration struggle another four years to gain terms no better than the United States might have had in 1968 or even 1967.

# CHAPTER THREE

# *Carter's Election, Vance's Appointment*

The election of James E. (Jimmy) Carter to the presidency in 1976 came at a special moment in the post–World War II era—the aftermath of the Vietnam War. Not only was Vietnam perhaps the first major military defeat in American history and a blow to the national pride, but it was attended by a bitterly divisive political debate and by revelation of wrongdoing on the part of administrations going back to that of Kennedy. Generational differences, a lessened commitment to polity, loss of self-discipline, stress on personal and material well-being at all levels of society, decline in belief that government was doing the job—all contributed to what was nothing less than a national loss of will. Critics drew the lesson that Vietnam had demonstrated the limits of America's power, that the world was contracting, and that the dynamics of change were becoming more difficult to control. Opponents said the war could have been won and argued that only the will had been lacking, undermined by the appeasers.

The Vietnam War shattered the post-1945 foreign policy consensus and gave rise to three widely different views on American foreign relations. One, labeled "Cold War internationalism," considered the Soviet Union still the greatest threat to American security and world peace. Its adherents believed that America must remain militarily superior and be willing not just to contain Russia, but to challenge the Soviet system. Another view has been labeled "post-

Cold War internationalism": it looked on the Soviet Union as a competitor, but not the only or even the most significant problem facing the United States. Americans had to confront many problems, not all caused by the Soviet Union, and recognize that the ability to control them had been reduced by loss of economic power and by the sharply reduced usefulness of military might for dealing with Third World conflicts. A third belief, opposed to interventionism and represented prominently by diplomat-historian George F. Kennan and by Senator George McGovern, argued that the United States ought to shift the emphasis to avoid any more Vietnams, contributing what it could to conflict resolution and international order. The existence of these three conflicting outlooks in Congress after 1972 made bipartisan support of any single policy all but impossible.[1]

The foreign policy of President Richard M. Nixon and his Secretary of State, Henry A. Kissinger, had sought to re-establish a consensus and at the same time maintain America's primacy in the face of loss of nuclear superiority. By pursuing both the war in Vietnam and détente, the Nixon administration had sought to salvage the nation's prestige while reducing costs associated with the Cold War, and to shift more of the containment burden to allies and clients. It tried to retain America's hegemony without repeating the mistake of Vietnam.[2] The Nixon-Kissinger strategy succeeded for a while, but in the end failed to save South Vietnam, which fell to Hanoi in 1975. Détente's political and diplomatic benefits were not as great as its supporters had expected.

Carter won the early Democratic primaries of 1976 largely because of absence of a front-runner and because of disenchantment of voters with Washington-based politicians, but also because of the confusion over foreign policy. Carter was "perhaps all too faithfully a man of the season—the season of confusion in U.S. foreign policy goals following the country's misadventure in Vietnam."[3] And just as there was no consensus within the Republican party, so there was no consensus among Democratic regulars, divided between the McGovern wing, advocating a return to virtual isolationism, and the wing of Senator Henry M. Jackson that was so distrustful of the Soviets as to be unacceptable to liberals. Senator Edward Kennedy's candidacy was mortgaged by the tragedy of Chappaquiddick.

It was this situation that permitted Carter to enjoy the advantage of an outsider. He could promise the country he would reform Washington; unlike Nixon and Kissinger he would have an open administration. Much of the public, sickened by Vietnam, and reeling also from the Watergate fiasco and revelations not merely about the presidency but about such sacrosanct government agencies as the Central Intelligence Agency, wanted a return to the ideal view of America's role. And even Carter supporters were surprised by the vein of political gold they had struck with Carter's human rights emphasis. While the country had lost much of its infatuation with détente, there was also continued support for the Strategic Arms Limitations Talks, the centerpiece of détente. Carter promised to go Kissinger one better in this regard. Limiting nuclear arsenals to existing levels was not enough; he would settle for nothing less than sharp reduction. Taking advantage of disenchantment with the military, he promised to cut military spending, already below its Vietnam level. Above all he tapped the idealism of the American people with his neo-Wilsonian rhetoric calling for respect for the right of all peoples to self-determination and to human decency, open covenants openly arrived at, an end to secrecy and force in foreign policy, a ringing reassertion of confidence in American-style democracy. He summed up his program in a commencement address of 1977 at the University of Notre Dame:

> I believe we can have a foreign policy that is democratic, that is based on fundamental values, and that uses power and influence, which we have, for humane purposes. We can also have a foreign policy that the American people support and for a change know and understand. . . . Because we know that democracy works we can reject the arguments of those rulers who deny human rights to their people.
>
> We are confident that the democratic methods are most effective, and so we are not tempted to employ improper tactics at home or abroad.
>
> We are confident of our own strength, so we can seek substantial nutual reductions in the nuclear arms race.
>
> . . . we are free of that inordinate fear of Communism which once led us to embrace any dictator who joined us in fear.
>
> For many years we've been willing to adopt the flawed and erroneous principles and tactics of our adversaries. But through failure [Vietnam] we have now found our way back to our own principles and values.

It was a philosophy, unfortunately, that was difficult to sustain. Détente had been carried by a combination of *Realpolitik* and public relations. Already public opinion favored more military spending and a tougher line toward the Kremlin. It was one thing to level with the public and quite another to convince people of the merits of policies, especially if policies appeared soft on the Soviets. And the convincing was not made easier by Carter's personality, which was an awkward combination of traits.

Carter's all-pervasive moralism seemed to color every aspect of the campaign. His brand of moralism was inspired by belief in man's ability through God's mediation to become a better person. Neither a moralism inspired by dour Calvinism nor by bleak intolerance, it has been described as that of a man "who fastens onto pieces and parts of life that have become heavily moralized, usually by a religious community, [leaving] whole swatches of important areas of human living untouched."[4] Admittedly it was "better than slipping into the morass of the amoral and immoral elimination of standards. A stiff necked moral simplicity is at least a corrective to cynicism and can be made effective symbolically."[5] But it has its limits. It may create a false picture of the realm in which choices have to be made. The moral striver, "shaping his life around his list of promises and resolutions, has a hard time avoiding the thought he is better than others . . . all the others that do not behave as he does."[6]

When to this was joined a view of political leadership as management, an outlook that had marked Carter's performance as governor of Georgia, that too was bound to effect his presidency. As William Lee Miller notes, the moralist and manager alike were standing apart from qualities that make for political leadership:

I mean "political" here in the deep and proper sense. . . . The moralizer (the conscientious man striving to fulfill the plain dictates of right and wrong) and the manager (the competent man trying to straighten out the world and make it more efficient, predictable and reorganized) share an implicit picture of human history and society that does not take fully into account the perennial ingredients of politics: conflicting interests, struggle for power, and differences in value among groups.[7]

Carter would be an outsider to Washington in a double sense. He was a moralist in a city where the prevalent philosophy is scepticism, if not cynicism. He was also imbued by the values or ideas of an engineer-manager without the charisma or ability to project the aura of leadership that so many Americans look for in a president. As a result, he would not be in a strong position to win the political support of the Congress, which would be indispensable to the success of his policies.

Vance's relationship with Carter prior to the latter's appointment as Secretary of State had not been close. They had formed an acquaintanceship only. The man whom Carter appointed his Assistant for National Security, Zbigniew Brzezinski, had been associated with Carter over several years, first in the so-called Trilateral Commission, an international private group that examined foreign policy questions and sought solutions, which then were sufficiently publicized that governments often were forced to take notice. Brzezinski was the American side's executive director. He was also in the campaign. Impressed by what he saw of the Georgia governor at the Kyoto meeting of the Trilateral Commission in the summer of 1975, he had gone out of his way to assist Carter.

Vance's association did not begin until after his own presidential candidate, Shriver, had withdrawn from the race. Among Carter's advisers in Atlanta, however, were such Vance acquaintances as Anthony Lake, Richard Holbrooke, and Richard Gardner. In the fall of 1976, at Carter's request, Vance prepared a memorandum setting out goals and priorities for a Carter foreign policy. It was not surprising, then, that after dining together on the night of the election, the Brzezinskis and Vances should have left the Gardners' New York apartment with some sense that their personal destinies were tied to the newly elected president.

When Carter's inner circle started considering cabinet appointments, Hamilton Jordan reportedly remarked that "if, after the inauguration, you find a Cy Vance as Secretary of State and Zbigniew Brzezinski as head of National Security, then I would say we failed. And I'd quit." No doubt some antipathy toward the foreign policy establishment existed among Carter loyalists. Fortunately, however, the secretaryship of state is one post that cannot be left to whims, ideological or otherwise. According to Brzezinski, with whom Carter discussed the matter, there were only three contenders—George Ball, Vance, and Paul Warnke, each a lawyer and recognized foreign policy expert, each with strong Democratic credentials. There is no reason to doubt Brzezinski's statement that by the time he had finished analyzing the three men for Carter he had strengthened Vance as Carter's choice. Vance fitted Carter's idea of the kind of person he wanted in that position: the New York lawyer was representative of the establishment yet not identified with its Vietnam disaster. Brzezinski has written of Vance as representative of the "once dominant WASP elite whose values had declining relevance to domestic and global realities." This is not the way he saw Vance at the time of his appointment. To his diary he confided: "I feel very good about Cy's selection."[8]

In relating Vance's appointment one cannot overlook the extent to which the foreign policy establishment centered in New York and Washington was in the throes of re-examination of the Vietnam premises that had taken for granted America's hegemony. A good sample of changing attitudes among the elite is provided in the 600 questionnaires returned at this time by a thousand presidents and vice presidents of the nation's five hundred largest corporations.[9] A majority believed that the threat of communism had decreased over the preceding decade, and three fifths chose trade, technical cooperation, and interdependence as the most important future approaches to peace. The priorities of American capitalists had undergone change; the stakes of foreign policy were more closely identified with economic than Cold War issues. Vance's campaign memorandum to Carter of October 1976 reflected this outlook:

> Although of importance, U.S.–Soviet issues should not be permitted to so dominate our foreign policy that we neglect relationships with our allies and other important issues, as has been the case in the past. Our principal goal must be to bring about continuing reduction of tension.[10]

Vance also represented the Democratic party's traditional combination of internationalism and idealism. Carter's platform and campaign positions were congenial. He shared Carter's call for a principled approach. Carter's views on issues, "although largely unformed, were in the centrist mainstream in which I felt comfortable."[11] Carter's emphasis upon the qualities of America and on the need to take initiative in promoting change were much in line with

Vance's thinking. It was not in Vance's nature to state objectives in such unqualified terms, but both men appeared to share the view that America's leadership would be strengthened by greater attention to diplomacy and international law.

When Carter invited Vance to Plains, Georgia, on November 30 and, after an evening's tour d'horizon, offered the post of Secretary of State, Vance had every reason to return to New York eager to break the momentous news to his wife and let his partners know he would soon be leaving the firm.[12]

When the Carter administration took office in January 1977, the country rightly had the impression that its three architects of foreign policy—the President, Vance, and Brzezinski—shared a philosophy. All three had been members of the Trilateral Commission. Carter and Vance were advocates of arms control. All three called for recognition of global interdependence. All three called upon America to regain leadership by showing respect for human rights and moral principle. Brzezinski had written *Between Two Ages: America in the Technetronic Era*, in which he argued that as the world came increasingly under the influence of communication and technology, in which the United States excelled, America would enjoy an ascendancy that the Soviet Union could never match.

Carter's messianic temper reinforced this euphoric view. The new President's foreign policy was to be the outward expression of inner grace, based on a conviction that the world could be redeemed by faith and works. While neither Vance nor Brzezinski made a great to-do of their religious faith, they shared Carter's idealism. In the Trilateral Commission, Carter may have found a secular .expression of do-goodism to complement his Christianity. The commission's celebration of interdependence and its call for cooperation and transformation had provided a model if not a philosophy of foreign affairs, reformist zeal, a vision of redemption—a perfect expression of Carter's call that it is a new world but America should not fear it.[13] Carter appointees believed that if America was to have a successful foreign policy it must be true to its better self, its higher ideals. It must no longer let anticommunism shape conduct. The United States could not act honorably, could not give attention to a more just international order, if it let itself be obsessed by the Soviet Union. Were we not ahead of the U.S.S.R.? What could Russia do for other countries that we could not? Our national security was often defined in terms of military competition with the Soviet Union. Such competition involved issues that could lead to war. But it could not be our preoccupation. These views, also expressed during the presidential campaign, were intended to prepare the American people for a new departure in foreign relations.

# CHAPTER FOUR

# *Secretary of State*

Carter's choice of Vance was not surprising, for of the candidates he seemed the most suitable, both politically and personally. The President needed an experienced adviser and negotiator with whom he could have an easy relationship. When asked for his recommendation, Brzezinski described him as "a team player who would fit well into my . . . model of a balanced leadership in the area of foreign affairs."[1] The New Yorker's attractions were equally real from a political standpoint. He stood well in the foreign policy establishment, with Congress and with the Democratic party—he was anything but an outsider. He had a quiet and unaggressive demeanor—quite the opposite of George Ball. Not that Vance was to prove shy; another insider who thought he knew Vance well from Pentagon days was astounded by Vance's incisiveness in defining issues and carrying them with colleagues, including the President.[2]

Carter determined to put his stamp on policy, and he was looking for a Secretary of State in the form of a collaborator. He planned to work through a system for decisions that called for collegiality.[3] Within this setup, Vance would be the President's foreign policy adviser and the Department of State would provide backup in policy preparation. In Carter's proposed system the Assistant for National Security would also serve as an adviser and provide policy coordination. In place of the highly centralized system that had developed under Nixon and Kissinger, two committees were created under the National Security Council—one chaired by Vance, the other by Brzezinski. Vance chaired the Policy Review Committee (PRC), which would have responsibility for recommendations on all matters of a diplomatic nature, while Brzezinski headed the Special Coordination Committee (SCC) to deal with "specific cross-cutting issues of national security requiring coordination among departments in the development of options" and in crisis management. Such a division required collegiality in which the Secretary of State would not be undercut by the Assistant for National Security, and this would depend, as Carter may have intended, upon the President relying upon his Secretary of State for final decisions.[4] As Vance later wrote, "A shared interest in all major policy problems is to be expected in a collegial system, but some understandings must also be developed to regulate initiative, consultation, the articulation of disagreements (without letting them become public) and the formulation of collective judgment."[5] Carter evidently counted on the fact that he, Vance, and Brzezinski would respect each other enough to achieve collegiality. Much would depend on team effort.

It would be naive to assume that Vance was not aware of Brzezinski as a possible rival in the collegial system. The fates of Rusk, frequently overshadowed by Bundy and McNamara, and of Secretary of State William P. Rogers, almost obscured by Kissinger, were recent reminders. Vance's concern was aroused by the organizational authority Brzezinski arrogated. But when aides drew it to his attention upon arrival in the department offices after Carter's inauguration, he downplayed this concern, remarking that he was not going to have collegiality compromised by mistrust from his side. A secure person, confident of his knowledge and experience, he did not feel the need to make an issue of bureaucratic turf. He was more disturbed a week later by Carter's decision that recommendations from the PRC and SCC were to be submitted directly to the President by the National Security Adviser without first being seen by the principals, namely, the Secretary of State and the Secretary of Defense. He was sufficiently prescient to recognize the power this gave Brzezinski to slant the summary of discussions and recommendations. Vance later reported that when he did get to see Brzezinski's summaries he found discrepancies, "occasionally serious ones, from my own recollection of what had been said, agreed, or recommended."[6] The integrity of the arrangement depended on each party observing collegiality.

Instead of worrying about collegiality, Vance undertook to make his department responsive to the President's needs. Carter had called for a break with the personal diplomacy of the Nixon-Kissinger administration. The professionals in the department welcomed the Carter-Vance philosophy and responded to Vance's leadership. In line with his view that everything must be done to make the department responsive, rather than ignoring his colleagues and doing everything himself, Vance sought courageous and creative assistants who would work with foreign service officers to develop policy according to administration values.

As his deputy Vance appointed Warren Christopher, whose abilities would come to public attention in the hostage crisis. As undersecretary for political affairs he called into service the veteran foreign service officer, Habib, with whom he had worked in the Vietnam negotiations. Other foreign service men appointed at the assistant secretary level included Arthur Hartman (Europe), Alfred Atherton, who had been Kissinger's roving ambassador (Middle East), Terence Todman (inter-American affairs), Harold Saunders (intelligence and research), and William Shaufele (African affairs).[7] To give the department the thrust that Carter's election called for, he appointed outsiders—some with experience, some not. Anthony Lake, who had courageously resigned from Kissinger's staff in protest over the invasion of Cambodia, was appointed head of the policy planning staff. Leslie Gelb, an experienced Washington hand, organizer of the Pentagon Papers and national security reporter for the *New York Times*, became director of political-military affairs. Patricia Derian, a Mississippi civil rights activist, was appointed Assistant Secretary for human rights; Andrew Young, permanent representative to the United Nations; Lucy Benson, head of the League of Women Voters, Undersecretary for security assistance; Richard Cooper, Yale provost and economist, Undersecretary for economic affairs; and Warnke, director of the Arms Control and Disarmament Agency and principal negotiator for SALT II. The appointment of Warnke was difficult because his outspoken reputation in favor of arms control had made him a target of the foes of détente in the Senate, but Vance determined to have him because of his experience as both a lawyer and negotiator. Almost all these appointments, and particularly that of Warnke, challenged the image of the State Department as a "fudge factory"—so much so that Senate approval of Warnke came only after a debate that marked the right-wing's initial assault upon any proposed policy of negotiating with the Soviet Union. Last but not least, Hodding Carter was appointed spokesman for the department. Vance counted on him to carry the ever heavier burden of communicating with the public.

Unlike his predecessor Rusk, not to mention Rogers, Vance had a strong relation to the department. As mentioned, he sought the advice of his colleagues, rather than bypassing them. And he gave the time to help his Undersecretary for management, Ben Read, carry through the Foreign Service Act of 1980, enhancing the pecuniary and professional attractiveness of the service. Vance also helped the department avoid delay. "If there was no decision to be taken then why were we bothering him?" was often his question to associates.[8] His experience with international realities was sufficient to give him a sense of the importance of forging ahead. In the case of one of his most important negotiations, the second phase of the Strategic Arms Limitation Talks (SALT II), this meant not mortgaging it to Soviet activities in, say, the Horn of Africa, which would have opened up endless speculation and endless possibilities for delay.

As for the Secretary of State's ideas about diplomacy, Vance acquired the reputation, principally from people in the National Security Council staff, of not having a conceptual mind. Anyone who has read his book, *Hard Choices*, will encounter a certain disparagement toward self-proclaimed conceptualizers. In some ways this put him at a disadvantage vis-à-vis Brzezinski. The President, a neophyte in foreign policy, was intrigued by Brzezinski's fine-spun presentations. By putting issues into a geopolitical frame Brzezinski gave Carter the impression he understood them better. Carter enjoyed listening to Brzezinski bounce his ideas off the walls of the Oval Office.

What might be seen as a weakness in this area was compensated for by a special strength. Vance had what for a better term might be called a policy mind. He had not engaged in the practice of trial law for twenty years without acquiring a feel for what was important in a situation. If Brzezinski was the master of the logico-deductive process—of deducing options from assumptions—Vance was the master of realistic assessment. His forte was identifying elements of a situation and determining what choices were workable.[9] He shunned giving Carter ideas merely for speculative effect. He recognized Carter's susceptibility, but considered issues too dangerous, especially speculative premises about Soviet motives or theoretical assumptions about America's credibility. Vance preferred to deal with policy in all its complexity.

In one respect Vance did differ from the President in regard to policy. Carter had come to office with a belief that America must no longer let the incubus of anticommunism deform policy. The United States, Carter contended, must slough off preoccupation with Russia, which like a malignant spirit was a curse to the nation's serenity:

> Our national security was often defined exclusively in terms of military competition with the Soviet Union. This competition is still critical, because it does involve issues which could lead to war. But however important this relationship of military balance, it cannot be our sole preoccupation, to the exclusion of other world issues which also concern us.[10]

Far from downgrading the centrality of the Soviet Union, as Carter had frequently called for in speeches, Vance continued to view the superpower relationship as crucial. The fact that the Soviet relationship was competitive and therefore difficult and potentially dangerous required that he manage it in as nonconfrontational a way as possible. He had a more sober view of Soviet motives than did Kissinger. He did not hope for superpower global co-dominion or accord on all issues. He was convinced that nuclear arms control was the one issue on which Soviet self-interest was as great as ours.

Vance, Carter, and Brzezinski seemed to share a view of the international system—the so-called "world order" model—that had been emerging among academics and had found partial expression in the Trilateral Commission. This was the view that as Europe and Japan had recovered from the war and as Third World countries achieved their independence, the world had become complex, pluralistic, and interdependent. "It is a new world, but America should not fear it. It is a new world, and we should help shape it. It is a new world that calls for a new American foreign policy."[11]

What Carter's euphoria masked was the fact that America's world hegemony was at an end. In the face of economic competition from Europe, Japan, and industrializing countries of the Third World, American leadership was becoming difficult. The Nixon administration's abandonment of the Bretton Woods monetary system, and the attempt by mercantilist means (exploiting its residual economic power to enhance its politcal power and vice versa) to pass economic costs of global hegemony along to allies, had only succeeded in postponing the issue of America's declining power. "Attempts to juggle competing domestic and international claims fueled a mounting inflation that both weakened the American economy and fed dissension within the world system."[12] This was the dilemma the Carter administration never resolved. But at least the "world order" approach had the merit of recognizing that changes in the rest of the world demanded attention fully as much as the East-West struggle. Further, instead of remaining passive the United States could serve its interest by attempting to shape this pluralistic world. The problem for Vance was how to realize this vision. The failure of military means in Vietnam placed a premium on diplomatic means, upon international law and perhaps even morality.

Brzezinski seemed even more ardent than Carter and Vance in sharing this world view. He published a book about the technetronic era in which he prophesied the decline of the Soviet Union as a global challenger and the demise of Soviet communism as an ideological force.[13] Rivalry with the United States was likely to continue, he wrote, "even if tempered by growing recognition that increased United States–Soviet collaboration is dictated by the basic imperatives of human survival," even if the combination of intensifying nationalism and eroding ideology made it unlikely that the Soviet Union would advance world revolution.[14] The Soviet system was static and stalemated, without the creativity to match the dynamic technological change of America.[15] The era of Communist revolution sponsored and controlled by Moscow was over, the Soviet record mixed, "hardly sufficient to justify the argument that only the Communists have the key to effective modernization."[16] As in the case of the Peoples' Republic of China, "future revolutions will be nationalist revolutions and expressions of nationalist communism. Hence the revolutions to come will neither signify an auto-

matic addition to 'international communism' nor represent a step
forward toward the intellectual unity of mankind."[17] Of the implications Brzezinski wrote: "An American-Soviet axis is not likely to be
the basis for a new international system; traditional spheres of
influence are increasingly unviable . . . an extensive American
military presence abroad is becoming counterproductive to American interests and to the growth of an international community . . .
Although American foreign policy has not been undifferentiated by
anti-communism as its critics . . . assert, there has been a strong
rhetorical tendency in American official circles to reduce international problems to an ideological confrontation and to identify
radical change as contrary to American interests . . . As the gradual
pluralization of the communist world continues to accelerate, this
will reduce reliance on active American intervention," making it
imperative to limit intervention to concrete American interests or in
response to overt hostile acts.[18] America's "credibility" as world
leader appeared secure in Brzezinski's 1970 book.

While Vance was not likely to express himself in such an unbut-
toned fashion, he recognized that world change had many indigenous aspects and ought not to be viewed simply as an expression of
the East-West conflict. He envisaged a diplomatic role for the
United States in conflicts where her interests were at stake, not
waiting for history to validate American superiority.

Below the surface were critical differences between the two men,
which were to affect the administration's policy. Leaving aside the
part that personality, confusion, and politics were to play in the
Carter administration, one could note the difference in their views
of the Third World, and of the Soviet Union.

Vance took the view that nationalism confronted both America
and the Soviet Union. "The diversity and irrepressible thirst for
national freedom among the world nations are the surest barricade
to foreign domination. We can best protect our interests . . . by
welcoming this diversity and respecting this spirit."[19] He had a
robust confidence in Third World nationalism and its capacity to
limit Soviet influence. Cuba excepted, there was ample evidence
that the Soviets could rarely create an alliance or establish a position
threatening to American security. Except where the Red Army
imposed itself, Soviet influence was reversible.    As Deputy Secre-

tary of Defense, Vance had watched the nation justify intervention in Vietnam to contain Communist China, only to have Nixon and Kissinger end up wooing Moscow and Beijing to contain North Vietnam. He had watched a war pursued to maintain America's credibility destroy that credibility. This convinced him that the Third World ought not to be viewed in terms of superpower competition and that in the search for self-determination, Third World states would not let themselves become tools of Russia. Military intervention ought to be the last and least-employed means. He was especially skeptical of abstract approaches reduced to glib metaphors like "arc of crisis"—that brought memories of falling dominoes.

Brzezinski, however, saw an increasingly fragile Western system open to Soviet intervention unless checked by American power. His technetronic world view in which American leadership was foreordained had been shadowed by the Spenglerian cast of Kissinger's view. The contemporary situation, he averred, reflected an end to a "long chapter in the history of the West, namely the West's predominance."[20] Brzezinski, Vance, and Carter all accepted global complexity and the inevitability of change. Carter and Vance were prepared to see the beneficent side of change. Brzezinski beheld change as conflict and turmoil from which the Soviet Union stood to gain.

A similar divergence marked Vance's and Brzezinski's views of the Soviet Union. Vance thought it important but not all-important, and refused to link it with general troubles, of an indigenous nature, around the world. Brzezinski disagreed; as early as 1976, in a memorandum to Gardner, he had argued that the U.S. must "strive to make détente both more *comprehensive* and more *reciprocal*."[21] Those would become code words for linkage between Soviet behavior in Africa and elsewhere and progress on SALT II. Soviet interest, Brzezinski declared, was to keep détente

> limited and rather one-sided. In fact, the Soviets so interpret it quite explicitly . . . the Soviet leaders have openly stated that détente is meant to promote the 'world revolutionary process' and they see Soviet-American détente . . . as a way of creating favorable conditions for the acquisition of power by Communist parties, especially given the so-called aggravated crisis of capitalism.[22]

After the Soviets' rejection of the administration's proposal for deep cuts in nuclear arsenals, Brzezinski confided in his diary that "neither Carter nor his other advisors appreciate the degree to which the Soviets are hostile . . . and the extent to which they wish to put us under pressure."[23]

Inevitably these divergent views of Soviet plans and opportunities led to divergent recommendations. Vance argued that despite the competitiveness of Soviet-American relations, the United States had interest in a strategic arms limitation agreement, and that it was not in American interest to link such an agreement to Soviet behavior in other areas. While Vance acknowledged the competitive element in Soviet policy, he rejected the argument that activities in Africa and elsewhere were part of a grand design of global expansion. The Kremlin's behavior was opportunistic, to gain influence and secure recognition, when and where it could, as a a superpower. Brzezinski argued that détente must be reciprocal. The willingness of Moscow to link behavior on other issues to arms negotiations should be a test of sincerity, and he proposed slowing SALT II both to press the Russians and reassure domestic critics.

The two men disagreed on instruments of policy. Consistent with the administration's view that the primary cause of revolution and local conflict lay in indigenous factors, Vance argued that the appropriate response was to try to remedy those conflicts either through diplomacy or the help of allies and other parties, not to attempt in futile fashion, to eliminate Soviet influence. This conviction expressed the need to work with change rather than oppose it; among Third World nations the desire for independence would guard against Soviet subversion.

Overlooked was the remarkable extent to which some Carter policies represented a continuation of those laid down by Kissinger, under congressional and public pressure, in his final two years. Continuity was not apparent in Carter's initial approach to SALT II, where his call for deep cuts departed from Kissinger's Vladivostok terms. But other Carter policies did demonstrate continuity—such as the decision to push the Panama Canal Treaty, which Kissinger had shelved because of pressure from the radical right led by Governor Ronald Reagan of California; likewise the effort to restore movement to Middle East policy, by working for a new Geneva

Conference and by the Camp David Accords—the latter a return to Kissinger's step-by-step diplomacy. Vance's diplomacy toward Zimbabwe and southern Africa, a success in part because it picked up where Kissinger had left off, dealt with political forces not as part of the East-West struggle (although a settlement was to America's strategic benefit), but in terms of indigenous realities. The policy of normalizing relations with the Peoples' Republic of China was also an effort to complete a process begun by Nixon and Kissinger, which had run out of steam when President Gerald Ford had to confront criticism within his own party.

Even on some of the more esoteric issues such as the Ford administration's last-minute efforts to establish better control over nuclear proliferation, Carter policy represented continuity. And, of course, the negotiation of the Tokyo Round of tariff reductions, started under the Ford administration, maintained an open and expanding international economy.

In keeping with the continuity that great power diplomacy requires, the Carter administration brought energy and vision to policies that had been forgotten or shelved as Kissinger's one-man show began to flag. Keeping the pressure on everywhere, the Carter administration believed, would reduce troubles between Russia and America and the likelihood of violence and guerrilla war in the Middle East and southern Africa.

# CHAPTER FIVE

# SALT II *(Part One)*

The danger of nuclear war, or even of a runaway arms race, was a concern so compelling that it transcended arguments about the behavior or intentions of the Soviet regime. It was the one aspect of Soviet-American relations that could not be linked to other aspects, the one area that had to be insulated from damaging blows. Still, any agreement with the Soviets had to be verifiable, if it was to deserve support of Congress.

The Kremlin, too, seemed determined to ignore whatever interpretations might be placed upon Soviet-American relations elsewhere. Premier Leonid Brezhnev had made several concessions to the American position at the Vladivostok meeting with Ford and Kissinger in November, 1974. Unlike the SALT I interim agreement of 1972, which permitted the Soviet Union a numerical advantage in intercontinental and sea-launched ballistic missiles (ICBMs, SLBMs), Vladivostok called for an aggregate ceiling of 2,400 for all strategic delivery vehicles (missiles, bombers) and a subceiling of 1,320 for MIRVed launchers—that is, launchers containing multiple, independently targeted reentry vehicles, or warheads. At Vladivostok the United States had dropped insistence on reductions in Soviet large-thrust ICBMs (set at 308) in return for Soviet agreement to U.S. forward-based systems, namely, nuclear-armed land- and carrier-based aircraft stationed in Western Europe. The Soviets refused to agree to limits on their Backfire bomber, which they insisted was not a strategic weapon, and the U.S. had resisted limits on cruise missiles—jet-powered, terrain-guided drones equipped with nuclear warheads.

There is now considerable evidence that Brezhnev succeeded in meeting the American terms at Vladivostok only after a prolonged struggle within the regime to overcome not only opposition from the military but from party hardliners opposing greater reliance on economic relations and détente with the West.[1] According to one observer, "Brezhnev badly needed to pick up momentum in foreign policy . . . controversies in the Soviet polity had reached the point where American credibility regarding détente had become a yardstick by which to measure Brezhnev's policy."[2] Brezhnev had only with difficulty been able to sustain his version of détente because "the top leadership within the Politburo closed its ranks against the mounting opposition to Brezhnev's policy in general, and to its economic and ideological consequences in particular" coming from party bureaucrats and economic managers.[3] In the period following Vladivostok, he had gone so far as to predict a new summit and a SALT II agreement by the end of 1975.[4] His position was greatly weakened by the Ford administration's decision to postpone a summit until after the elections. He continued to defend his thesis that limiting the risk of nuclear war through arms control was to Soviet interest. "Beginning with a speech by Brezhnev in Tula in January 1977, Soviet official discourse shifted openly to embrace the concept of strategic balance. Brezhnev denied that superiority was an objective of Soviet policy; in subsequent statements, he posited "parity" and "approximate equilibrium" as the goals of Soviet defense policy.[5] We know now also that although Soviet military spending had grown by an annual rate of 4 to 5 percent during the early 1970s, it had begun to level off at 2 percent for the period after 1976.[6]

When Carter came into office, a disagreement at once developed within the administration over the approach to SALT II. Vance preferred to take advantage of the political strength of the new administration, the traditional honeymoon with Congress, to attempt an agreement based on Vladivostok, which would postpone the cruise missile and Backfire issues. He greatly admired Kissinger's achievement and wanted to maintain negotiation.[7] But neither Carter nor Brzezinski wanted to initiate arms control on the basis of Kissinger's accomplishments. Moreover, in the campaign, Carter had promised that he would not settle for limits but would pursue reductions. He desired deep cuts in the nuclear arms of both the U.S. and the U.S.S.R.

Confronted by a President determined to redeem a campaign pledge to reduce nuclear arsenals, Vance and his arms negotiator, Warnke, may have yielded too readily to Carter's call for deep cuts. At a crucial White House meeting on March 12, 1977, Carter voiced his impatience with "merely staying within the Vladivostok framework" and his interest in "a fundamentally new kind of proposal."[8] At this point Secretary of Defense Harold Brown appears to have asked for deep cuts that ostensibly would reduce the impending superiority of Soviet intercontinental missiles and thereby the danger that the Soviets might gain a first-strike capability. Brown's reasoning had such an appeal to Carter that it ended discussion.[9]

Vance and Warnke failed to emphasize the effect that by-passing Vladivostok would have on Moscow: reduction from 2,400 to 1,800 missiles, and from 1,320 MIRVed missiles to 1,100 or 1,200. The air-launched cruise missile range was set at 2,500 kilometers instead of 1,500, largely on Brown's recommendation. The Soviets were to be asked to limit their large-thrust missiles to 150. It was openly acknowledged that one purpose of deep cuts was to impose a one-sided reduction on Soviet intercontinental missiles so as to prevent first-strike capability. Brzezinski later wrote that Carter received a letter from Brezhnev on March 15 warning that SALT II "should be essentially a reflection of the Vladivostok understanding," but Carter and his advisers still went forward with their deep-cut proposal. The whole affair was concocted in a vacuum and did not become more widely known within the government until it was too late.

Brzezinski seems to have anticipated failure of the deep-cut strategy. In the privacy of his diary he admitted that to ask for deep cuts was hopeless. In his diary for March 25, 1977, he wrote:

> I expect that the Soviets will not accept our proffered offer . . . if however we can stand fast and not be intimidated and keep pressing, it is conceivable that the Soviets will come around . . . which in that case would mark a really significant turning point in the U.S.-Soviet relationship.[10]

For this reason he favored convincing the Soviets that "we were prepared to stand pat and if necessary, even to engage in an arms race."[11] If Brzezinski expected failure why, then, did he not warn Carter? In the meetings on March 19 and 22, he confined himself to analysis of options, and left complexities to Vance, who was given a fallback position, a less drastic set of cuts, to be used only to lessen the expected Soviet reaction.

The subsequent Moscow meeting was a fiasco from beginning to end, and opened the administration to charges of incompetence. The situation was made worse by Carter's decision to outline the new proposal in a speech to the U.N. General Assembly before Vance had even left for Moscow. This breach of confidentiality was another sore point with the ever-suspicious Soviet leadership, fearful of being put on the spot.

When Vance arrived in Moscow on March 27, it was not a storm in which he found himself, but a hurricane. The vehemence and finality with which the Kremlin rejected the American offer shocked him, although in Washington Ambassador Anatoly Dobrynin had warned him to expect rejection. Everything went wrong. There was not even a hint of a counterproposal. Carter refused to submit the fallback proposal. New to negotiating with the Soviets, Vance, prior to leaving Moscow, foolishly gave a press conference that violated the Soviet penchant for secrecy and drew bitter condemnation from Foreign Minister Andrei Gromyko.

Vance sought to put the best face possible on the fiasco. "My view," he reported to Carter,

> is that they have calculated, perhaps mistakenly, that pressure will build on us to take another position. One of their problems is that they feel we have departed too far from the basic Vladivostok framework. . . . In any case we should not be discouraged. A certain testing period was probably to be expected.[12]

Brzezinski was more satisfied with Soviet recalcitrance. "I think we can really put a lot of pressure on the Soviets," he wrote in his diary for March 30:

> We have developed an approach which is very forthcoming; on the one hand we are urging reductions, with the other hand we are urging a freeze, and at the same time we are urging more recognition for

human rights. All of that gives us a very appealing position, and I can well imagine that the Soviets feel in many respects hemmed in.[13]

In fact, the President's proposal had only given the Soviet leadership opportunity to vent its wrath. While Brzezinski was quietly expressing contempt for anyone weak-kneed enough to call for concessions, standing pat was not an option for Vance and his lieutenants, who now concentrated on finding a way to reopen negotiations. The Secretary of State also became a more assertive adviser. As he recalled his advice to the President: "In dealing with the Soviets we couldn't be as open as we had hoped we could. Out in the open is just not the way that they are prepared to negotiate."[14]

Vance thereafter determined to play a more careful role both in identifying a negotiable proposal and insulating it against competition in the other areas of Soviet-American relations. The Carter approach to SALT had not worked. He needed an alternative that would provide the basis for negotiation and be acceptable to an increasingly critical audience. "Carter's preoccupation with achieving some reductions in total number, admirable as that might be, would be offset if an agreement was not reached by the instability, strategic and political, of a runaway arms race."[15]

Any new proposal had to meet Carter's concern that there be reductions in both arsenals, not just dotting the "i"s and crossing the "t"s of Kissinger's Vladivostok accord, and deal with the concern of the joint chiefs of staff for both the Backfire bomber and Soviet intercontinental, large-thrust missiles, while leaving the U.S. free to deploy cruise missiles. Verifiability had to be assured, and the allies satisfied the U.S. was not bargaining away their nuclear umbrella.

Not only must the treaty stand on its merits—that is, meet the national interest of the United States—but it must be defensible against domestic critics. Science and technology constantly spawned new weapons; the Soviets had not only caught up, but their ability to mount six or even ten warheads on large rockets had created a strategic and political nightmare for arms controllers. Critics who would never have considered denying the United States the advantage of MIRVed launchers now trumpeted the charge that Soviet rockets with multiple warheads gave Moscow a first-strike capability against U.S. land-based missiles.

The need to be tough with the Russians in order to protect the President politically was emerging as a consideration.[16] The problem was to repackage the American proposal so as to win acceptability while achieving a verifiable treaty that would have some chance of Senate approval.

For a time Vance and Brzezinski were in nominal agreement, but each viewed the situation differently. While Vance saw progress on arms control as crucial to the U.S.-U.S.S.R. relationship, Brzezinski saw the Soviets as hostile, threatening the ability of the United States to stand up to Moscow in the early 1980s. While Vance sought terms that would both meet Soviet worries and assure nuclear security, Brzezinski was more concerned that the United States might want an agreement so badly that "we begin changing our proposals until the point is reached that the Russians are prepared to accept it."[17]

The repackaging was worked out in discussions with Leslie Gelb (State), William Hyland (NSC), and Walter Slocombe (Defense). To get around the disagreements on several weapons they devised a three-tier or three-stage approach. The first would be a treaty limiting missiles and bombers capable of launching cruise missiles to some number less than Vladivostok; the second an agreement for two or three years that would permit both sides to bypass the really difficult issues like cruise missiles; the third, a declaration of principles, was a commitment to deeper cuts and other qualitative limits (including forward-based systems) in a SALT III agreement. Since the United States had no plans to deploy ground- or sea-launched cruise missiles within immediately forthcoming years, accepting an interim ban would be painless. That left unsettled the issue of Soviet heavy missiles and the status of the Backfire bomber, and on the Soviet side how the number and range of the American air-launched cruise missiles were to be determined. Vance and Warnke raised these considerations first within the White House and then with Dobrynin. The discussions, Brzezinski writes, "paid off."[18]

This time Foreign Minister Gromyko was informed well in advance, and no upsetting public disclosures attended Vance's May 18 meeting with him in Geneva. The Soviet side was still unyielding on U.S. efforts to reduce Soviet heavy missiles below 300 (the U.S. sublimit was now 190 on MIRVed SS-18s instead of the earlier 150).

But Gromyko was willing to count a heavy bomber armed with air-launched cruise missiles as the equivalent of a multiple warhead, and as part of the 1,320 sublimit on all MIRVed warheads. The Soviets also accepted the American three-tier proposal with the suggestion that the proposed interim executive agreement on difficult issues be treated as a protocol to the treaty. The stage was thus set for full-time negotiators in Geneva to narrow the differences: whether the aggregate level of delivery vehicles would be 2,250 (the Soviet position) or 2,150 (U.S. position); whether the number of MIRVed vehicles should be 1,320 (Soviet side) or 1,200 (U.S.); whether air-launched cruise missile (ALCM) limits should be in the treaty (Soviet view) or in the protocol (U.S.); whether ALCM–carrying heavy bombers should count in the 1,320 (Soviet), versus a sublimit of 250 (U.S.); whether MIRVed heavy missiles should be limited to 190 (U.S. position); whether there should be a sublimit of 250 on the Backfire bomber (U.S. position); whether the ban on new ICBMs should apply only to MIRVed ICBMs (Soviet position) or all ICBMs (U.S.). Even more esoteric issues involving a ban on Soviet encryption of telemeters for testing missiles (essential to U.S. verification) and permissible changes in missile sizes and silos would have to be settled (the so-called modernization issue). Still, Vance could leave Geneva in May knowing that the SALT II negotiation was starting again.[19]

Unfortunately the delicate balance that the administration had achieved in the SALT negotiating package now was damaged by Carter's decision to cancel the B-1 bomber. Looking for ways to keep his pledge to reduce military spending, and persuaded by technical analysis, the President made his decision on cost-effectiveness. The B-1 was proving inordinately expensive, and B-52s with air-launched cruise missiles could do the job just as effectively. Defense hawks and anti-SALT II hardliners seized on the decision as evidence that the administration was "soft" on defense and practicing "unilateral" arms control. The effect of the decision might have been lessened had the administration used cancellation as a bargaining chip with the Soviets.[20]

By the time Vance and Gromyko were due to meet again in September 1977, the Geneva negotiations were still deadlocked on critical items, and Carter and Brzezinski were becoming irritated.

Rather than risk further delay, Vance proposed to take up issues when Gromyko arrived in New York for the annual opening of the U.N. General Assembly. The Soviets still refused to consider any reduction in heavy missiles and continued to argue that the 1,320 subceiling on MIRVed vehicles should include whatever B-52s the United States intended to equip with air-launched cruise missiles. Gromyko agreed to include ALCM-carrying heavy bombers in the 1,320 ICBM totals (since the United States had only 1,050 ICBMs, this would permit counting ALCM-armed B-52s as part of the 1,320 total), if the United States would drop its demand that the Soviets dismantle part of their 308 heavy missiles. He agreed that the Soviets would not give the Backfire capacity to operate at intercontinental distances, and would limit annual production. In a meeting with Carter, he agreed to accept a launcher ceiling of 2,250 (a reduction from Vladivostok of 150) and a ceiling of 1,320 for MIRVed launchers and ALCM–carrying bombers, 1,250 of which would be missiles (in opposition to a proposed U.S. ceiling of 1,200). Eventually Gromyko would agree to accept the U.S. limit of 1,200 MIRVed launchers (with a subceiling on MIRVed ICBMs of 820). This permitted the United States to count 120 of its ALCM–carrying B-52s as part of the 1,320 subceiling before they had to be counted against the MIRVed missile total.

The talks with Gromyko promised heartening progress, much of it in a direction favorable to American objectives, but unfortunately they encountered a combination of misrepresentation and attacks on the credibility of any agreements with the Soviet Union from Senator Jackson and from the Committee on the Present Danger, headed by Paul Nitze and Eugene Rostow. Consistent with the administration's promise to consult with the Senate on a regular basis, Vance testified on October 14, 1977, before Jackson's subcommittee on SALT II. He defended the provisions that would allow the U.S.S.R. to deploy up to 308 SS-18s and 19s on the ground that the accord would limit MIRVed land-based ICBMs to about 800 and not leave the United States any more vulnerable to a first strike than was the Soviet Union to an American first strike. Almost immediately the critics of détente led by Nitze attacked the accords because they would not provide for nuclear stability. Since the United States was still ahead in warhead numbers and likely to remain so, Nitze's

claim of imbalance was spurious; what he and his fellow critics
objected to was that the Soviet Union would be allowed to catch up.
The administration was constrained from going public with the
Soviet concessions because of the confidentiality of negotiations,
and by the desire not to appear to claim a propaganda victory.

Jackson and his aide Richard Perle now became the focus of
charges by a group of pro–arms-control senators of being the source
of damaging leaks and misrepresentations that were feeding the
anti-SALT campaign of the Committee on the Present Danger. The
letter from five senators asking the Armed Services Committee
chairman, John Stennis, to investigate the leaks, and that hearings
be taken from Jackson's subcommittee, poisoned the situation. A
Carter speech defending the SALT negotiations was then followed
by a Jackson attack on the administration.

The administration also had to defend the negotiations against
attack from an entirely different direction—the European allies.
Geographical and political differences between Europe and North
America and disparities in military power had been a source of
tension ever since the North Atlantic Treaty Organization was
established. Europeans did not want the United States to be so
provocative in relations with the U.S.S.R. as to risk nuclear war, but
they did not want the United States to neglect their security by a
Soviet-American deal. The West Germans also wanted to improve
East-West relations as the only means of healing the East-West
fracture of the German nation; France had competing interests; and
the alliance was not the only concern of the United States, which
had to balance its European problems against others, particularly in
the Middle East. Keeping European allies happy was always a
delicate matter, made even more delicate by shifts in national power
and leadership among the European nations—particularly France,
Britain, and West Germany. By the mid-1970s, West Germany had
replaced Britain as the pivotal state in the alliance and enjoyed
stable relations with France.

The timing of press leaks on the three-tiered approach, under
which ground- and sea-launched cruise missiles would have been
subject to a protocol postponing development for three years pending negotiations, raised suspicion that the United States would give
up deploying cruise missiles in Europe in exchange for a speedy

SALT II agreement. In fact there was never any such thought on Vance's part. Testing and deployment of ground- and sea-launched cruise missiles was several years away. He merely proposed to postpone the issue pending ratification of SALT II, after which he would make it a special agreement or part of the Mutual Balanced Force discussion—the latter disarmament talks between NATO and the Warsaw Pact nations had been under way for several years. The missiles thus might be part of a bargain involving theater nuclear weapons. Or they might eventually be deployed. The fact that Vance also retained the right to transfer cruise-missile technology to Europe, to the NATO allies, was lost in the attack by right-wing critics. Even more unfortunate, the matter was made a burning political issue by Chancellor Helmut Schmidt of West Germany in an October 1977 speech in London criticizing the failure of the United States to deal with Soviet deployment of SS-20s in Eastern Europe.

As mentioned, the late September 1977 meeting between Carter and Gromyko produced movement. The Soviets agreed to abandon any range limit on air-launched cruise missiles, permitting the United States to test and deploy at unlimited ranges. In return the United States accepted a 600-km range limit on ground-launched and submarine-launched cruise missiles, this in the protocol to the treaty. The Soviets would not give assurance against upgrading the Backfire, and still refused to certify its production rate, which the joint chiefs considered important. The United States countered by reserving the right to deploy an aircraft comparable to the Backfire. Gromyko disappointed Vance by returning to Moscow before he could complete a treaty.

A new snag then arose—the telemetry encryption issue. If the treaty was to be verifiable, the United States had to be able to monitor missile tests. The Soviets found it difficult to concede the right of the United States to monitor such tests. Gromyko refused to admit that telemetry had anything to do with the proposed treaty. The issue boiled down to a difference of emphasis, but a difference sufficiently sensitive that it needed language to bridge the positions. And this was not the end of technical issues, the resolution of which delayed the signing of a SALT II treaty for a year.

# CHAPTER SIX

# The Horn of Africa

Until the winter of 1977–1978 the difference in the way Vance and Brzezinski interpreted Soviet motives remained out of public print. In December 1977, however, Soviet activities in the Horn of Africa, a projection of the African land mass into the Red Sea and Indian Ocean, brought these interpretations into open conflict. The trouble arose in Somalia and Ethiopia, unlikely places for a test between two American advisers on foreign policy. In the Horn the Soviet Union had supported the regime of Siad Barre in Somalia, and thereby enjoyed naval facilities at the Red Sea port of Berbera. The Soviets had supported the aspiration of the Somalis to annex the Ethiopian province of the Ogaden. Then in September 1974, young officers of the Ethiopian Army overthrew the American-backed regime of Ethiopian Emperor Haile Selassie, which had been a medieval despotism, and after a factional struggle within the junta, known as the Dergue, the victor emerged as Colonel Mengistu Haile Mariam. The Dergue treated its opponents atrociously, and the United States gradually withdrew economic and military aid. Moscow and its Western Hemisphere supporter, Cuba, welcomed the new Ethiopian regime and set about courting its favor. All might have ended well, for the Soviets and Cubans, save for one impossible fact—that to support Ethiopia meant antagonism from Somalia. The two Communist outside powers could not have it both ways. For a few months Moscow and Havana thought they could have their cake and eat it. Siad Barre, determined to take advantage of the situation, launched a military campaign against Ethiopia. On

November 13, 1977, Somalia expelled all Soviet advisers, took back facilities granted the U.S.S.R. since 1962, and abrogated the 1974 Somali-Soviet treaty of friendship. The Mengistu regime in Addis Ababa turned in desperation to Moscow and Cuba, which saw no alternative to providing troops to drive the Somalians out of the Ogaden. In the first week of February 1978, elite Cuban infantry, with support of Soviet advisers, began a counteroffensive.

Here was a question on which Vance and Brzezinski would take sides. Should the United States support Somalia even though it was the aggressor? Ethiopia had the backing of the Organization of African Unity, which served to legitimize the role of Cuban and Soviet troops and advisers in Addis Ababa's defense.

Carter had made it a point of policy that however important was military competition in Soviet-American relations, it must not be "our sole preoccupation to the exclusion of other issues." Vance, too, had stood for this idea. He had taken Carter's injunction to mean that the United States should not meet every Soviet move. In the case of the Horn of Africa he was convinced the Soviets would not get far. He had no need to read textbooks on Third World nationalism to know that with rare exceptions—perhaps only Cuba—neither communism nor military intervention had brought the conquests that hardline American propagandists and geopoliticians had claimed. He was impressed by Soviet losses in Yugoslavia, mainland China, Egypt, and half a dozen other countries. In keeping with what he thought was the President's intention he believed that Americans should not allow themselves to "become so preoccupied with the Soviets that we lost sight of our basic policy objectives in Africa."[1] The Organization of African Unity had rejected the Somali claim to the Ogaden, in keeping with the principle that to change the border of one African state would jeopardize the territorial integrity of all. To support Siad Barre would put Washington at odds with African governments.

Brzezinski took the opposite view. Because the Soviets and Cubans were supporting Ethiopia he argued that the U.S. had a stake in supporting the Siad Barre regime in Somalia, which was actively seeking backing and military equipment for its invasion of the Ogaden. The Ethiopian regime of Mengistu had signed an arms supply agreement with the Soviets.

Coupled with the expansion of Soviet influence and military presence in South Yemen, it posed a potentially grave threat to our position in the Middle East, notably in the Arabian peninsula. . . . I was strengthened in my view by the repeated, like-minded expressions of concern by both Giscard [French President Giscard d'Estaing] and Sadat [Egypt's President Anwar el-Sadat], leaders with a refined strategic perspective.[2]

As the Somali invasion progressed, Addis Ababa turned increasingly to Moscow and Cuba for reinforcement, and the movement of Soviet and Cuban personnel deepened the conflict between Vance and Brzezinski. Brzezinski's private view expressed in his diary was that because "everyone is afraid of getting into a crisis, there is a general tendency to downplay the seriousness of the issue."[3] "You could almost sense the anxiety . . . when I mentioned the possibility of more direct action to make it impossible for the Soviets and Cubans not only to transform Ethiopia into a Soviet associate but also perhaps to wage more effective warfare against Somalia."[4] He invoked a litany of reasons why the United States could not afford to remain passive—the strategic danger to Saudi Arabia, loss of confidence among such allies as Egypt and the Sudan, and the negative effect upon domestic American politics. He proposed deployment of a carrier task force near Ethiopia and stepped-up military aid to the Somali government.

Vance opposed this counsel, as did Secretary of Defense Brown. How would a carrier force alter the situation? It would either be a bluff, or bring the United States into the conflict. The U.S. should continue to work for a political settlement that would make it possible for the Somalis to withdraw.

The upshot was that Carter agreed that Vance should continue diplomatic efforts to mobilize the African states against Soviet- or Cuban-backed intrusion into Somalia, while pressing Addis Ababa to halt at the border. No one—neither America's allies nor the neighboring African states—was willing to contribute to military intervention. Vance impressed upon the Soviets the damage that involvement was causing the U.S.–U.S.S.R. relationship. On February 14, Dobrynin assured him that the Ethiopian regime had promised that once the Somalis were out of the Ogaden, Ethiopian forces would not cross the Somali border. On February 16 the

President obtained Mengistu's agreement to receive David Aaron, Deputy Assistant for National Security. Aaron was to make clear that should Ethiopian forces invade Somalia, they would be adding one more enemy—the United States—to those they already had.[5] By late February there was every indication, despite the imminent collapse of the Somali invasion, that Ethiopia would respect the territory of its opponent.

It was at this point that the irrepressible Brzezinski threw caution to the winds and revealed publicly his disagreement with the Secretary of State. He determined to link the conflict in the Horn to what he considered the larger pattern of Soviet expansion. He carefully approached the chairman of the Democratic party's national committee, Robert Strauss, and Vice President Walter F. Mondale and asked for their support. Then on March 1 he went public with what he had been saying for weeks in background press briefings—that the Soviet role in Ethiopia was part of a threat to American interests in the Arabian peninsula and that Soviet actions would complicate the SALT II negotiations. At Vance's insistence the President immediately rejected the implication that the United States intended to link events on the Horn to progress on SALT. But the damage had been done.

Vance was visibly angry. He felt that by adhering to geopolitical abstractions Brzezinski had ignored not just the national interest in SALT, but the military disadvantages of any U.S. intervention. In his memoirs Brzezinski assigned the collapse of the U.S. position in Iran and the Soviet invasion of Afghanistan to the administration's failure to intervene in the Horn. It was an attractive theory. But neither at the time nor when writing his memoirs did he give any evidence of how the one move would have forestalled others. He asked of Secretary Vance, and later the readers of his book, simple acceptance of his theory at a level of geopolitical generalization that required an act of faith.

To make matters worse, President Carter then wobbled in support of Vance—perhaps without realizing that he wobbled. The day after Brzezinski went public, Carter announced at a press conference that Soviet presence in Ethiopia had violated certain principles. He did not reveal those principles, which presumably were part of the never resolved (and probably irresolvable) disagreement between Moscow and Washington as to rules of superpower competition in the Third World. The President also said at the conference that Soviet actions would "lessen the confidence of the American people . . . in the peaceful intentions of the Soviet Union [and] would make it more difficult to ratify a SALT agreement. . . . We don't initiate the linkage."[6]

At a meeting that same afternoon Vance rejected both Brzezinski's and Carter's imputation of linkage. If the United States accepted the essentially competitive nature of the U.S.–U.S.S.R. relationship and still wanted a SALT agreement, it could not make the latter conditional upon Soviet withdrawal from Third World involvements.

All this confusion, one must add, came at a most inopportune time, just when Vance's cautious diplomacy in Africa was yielding results. If the Assistant for National Security and the President had kept quiet and let Vance handle African matters, the administration justly could have claimed a very considerable success in its African policy. The Secretary of State had adhered to international law and the political realities that Carter had pledged to make the touchstone of policy. While fighting continued on a small scale for several months, Ethiopian and Cuban forces were too busy trying to suppress Eritrean liberation forces inside Ethiopia (the problems of African nations are never simple) to bother with invading Somalia. While keeping a brutal regime in power the Soviets were altogether unsuccessful in imposing a Soviet-style regime. The United States was free to move on to the task of acquiring bases in both Somalia and neighboring Kenya, foreshadowing the strategic needs that developed after the loss of Iran and the Soviet invasion of Afghanistan.

# CHAPTER SEVEN

# *The Middle East*

Nowhere was the Carter administration more determined to preserve American interests than in the Middle East—the United States could not ignore the Persian Gulf nor the risk of another Arab-Israeli war. The West was dependent on Middle East oil. Americans were committed to the security of the State of Israel.

Of the two concerns, the Israeli problem seemed at the outset more important, more pressing. It was, of course, a domestic political minefield, given the absolute value that the American Jewish community assigned to Israel. Presidents Eisenhower, Kennedy, and Johnson had sought to avoid any active involvement until crises erupted. After the 1973 war, that was no longer possible. Kissinger had been compelled to mediate after the 1973 Yom Kippur or October War. Here, too, would be continuity with what Kissinger had undertaken. But what the Carter administration undertook was far more sweeping and comprehensive than Kissinger's "shuttle diplomacy."

Kissinger had limited himself to mediating a cease-fire and a set of partial withdrawals. His diplomacy was never the initial step in the pursuit of a peace settlement; it was to cope with the threat of renewed hostilities. Highly personal, it was also effective only when it involved a bilateral setting. It did not attempt to come to grips with the Palestinian problem. And Kissinger's step-by-step diplomacy was "somewhat unrealistic in trying to isolate the Soviet Union and Western Europe from the substance of the negotiations."[1]

Vance had outlined recommendations on the Middle East in a memorandum to candidate Carter in October 1976:

> I continue to believe that we should nudge the situation along, but not take any strong initiative in the first several months which should be devoted to quiet diplomacy directed to building a base for resumption of serious settlement discussions. Ultimately I believe we should urge the parties to reach a general settlement to be carried out in stages.[2]

He had watched Kissinger's shuttle diplomacy with admiration but recognized, as had Kissinger, that it had reached the limit of its effectiveness. Kissinger had focused on disengagement in the form of interim agreements, but knew that the next administration would have to tackle the big issues—Arab recognition of Israel, return of territory taken by Israel in the 1967 war, a settlement for the Palestinians. He knew that progress on one could not be made without progress on all. The Israelis would not give up Arab territory occupied in the 1967 war or make concessions on the Palestinian issue unless the Arabs, including the Palestine Liberation Organization, showed themselves ready to recognize Israel. Vance viewed the Palestinian people as

> the central, unresolved human rights issue of the Middle East. The President and I were convinced that no lasting solution in the Middle East would be possible until, consistent with Israel's right to live in peace and security, a just answer to the Palestinian question could be found, one almost certainly leading to a Palestinian homeland and some form of self-determination.[3]

Unfortunately this was the one point that the Israelis had no intention of conceding. And refusal of the Palestine Liberation Organization to recognize Israel's right to exist played directly into Israel's hand.

Two Middle East specialists in the Department of State, Alfred Atherton and Harold Saunders, together with William Quandt on the NSC staff, had been asked to prepare a paper setting forth options for the NSC Policy Review Committee.[4] Saunders and Atherton had worked with Kissinger. They offered the President and Vance either a policy of slight involvement, which might save the administration the consequences of tackling such a controversial situation, or an activist approach in which case the administration would participate directly in negotiating and take the risk of failure. There was never any doubt what the choice would be. Carter and Vance considered the risk to American interests from another Arab-Israeli war too great to ignore the situation. Vance in particular was ready to pick up where Kissinger had left off.

In seeking a solution to the Arab-Israeli problem, Vance and the President opted for a comprehensive approach calling for reconvening the Geneva Conference, which had last met in December 1973. It would be attended by the Soviet Union and all other parties to the conflict. Inviting the Soviet Union was bound to be criticized, but was worth the risk, partly in recognition of Moscow's stake in the Middle East, partly to deter the Soviets from playing the role of spoiler. Vance did not assume that all issues would be negotiated in plenary sessions. Each issue would be negotiated first by the parties directly involved before it was brought before a plenary session for ratification. This was the only way the United States could hope to achieve a settlement acceptable to enough Arab states to have legitimacy. Vance and his associates recognized that it would be incredibly difficult, perhaps impossible, to overcome the hostility and insecurity of both sides, but if all pieces could fall into place, each party might see enough advantages to lift the legacy of humiliation felt by the Arabs and the isolation felt by the Israelis.

The Secretary of State did not assume that a reconvened conference would be where all negotiation would take place. Getting parties to attend a reconvened conference was part of a strategy that would first involve identifying each government's minimum terms for a Middle East settlement. Vance would engage in several rounds of negotiation designed to convince all parties of the seriousness of the administration's intentions. Only when maximum concessions had been made on each side would the United States make known its recommendations, with the object of bridging the gaps.

So complete was his determination to move ahead that Vance left for an exploratory round of talks in Middle Eastern capitals in February 1977. The result could not have seemed encouraging, especially when Yitzhak Rabin, the Labor party leader and Israeli prime minister, made plain that Israel would never accept an independent Palestinian state on the West Bank, arguing that such a state's real aim would be reconquest of Israel. Vance sensed a possibility of peace between Israel and its Arab neighbors on boundary and territorial issues. Rather than rush things he recommended that Carter meet Arab leaders and the Israeli prime minister but hold off on exerting any pressure for a settlement.

Hardly was the subsequent round of Washington visits begun than the election of a new Israeli government under Menachem Begin created another uncertainty.[5] Vance and his advisers, to be sure, cautioned themselves against assuming that Begin would be immovable. Had he not shown himself something of a pragmatist? Nevertheless, the defeat of the party that had governed Israel since its founding, together with the coming to power of the Likud coalition, represented more than just a reversal of Labor fortunes. It represented a harsher view of the Arabs, by leaders far more committed to Israeli rule on the West Bank.[6] Discussion in the Policy Review Committee meanwhile had established a set of principles for negotiation of substantive Middle East issues, on which Vance and Carter would seek each government's views and if possible approval prior to reconvening the Geneva Conference.

Begin made his position explicit on the eve of his arrival in Washington. He called for unbending opposition to a Palestinian state, and expressed every intention of increasing the number and size of Israeli settlements in the occupied territories. Vance took the position that the "peace and security" in return for "withdrawal" provisions of U.N. Resolution 242, in regard to the occupied territories, had been accepted by all—both Arabs and Israelis. He had to negotiate *as if* Begin could be persuaded to accept autonomy for the West Bank. Otherwise there would have been no Camp David and no Israeli-Egyptian treaty.

The ensuing negotiation was at the least interesting. Vance found Begin an "odd mixture of iron will and emotionalism . . . capable of endlessly adhering to the same positions while castigating the motives of his negotiating partners for failing to agree."[7] And Carter was never more courageous than in warning Begin that the West Bank must be on any agenda and that Israel's continued settlement of the West Bank foreclosed negotiation and must cease. The President also made clear that if the PLO publicly endorsed U.N. Resolution 242 and acknowledged Israel's right to exist, the U.S. would talk to the PLO.[8]

Vance then presented Begin with the administration's negotiating principles for a comprehensive peace conference:

1. that the final outsome of negotiation must take the form of treaties and not just agreements;
2. U.N. Resolutions 242 and 346 would be the basis of negotiation;
3. any settlement would require an end to belligerency and establishment of normal relations between Israel and its Arab neighbors;
4. there should be a phased withdrawal of Israeli forces on all fronts to secure borders, with appropriate security arrangements; and
5. there should be a Palestinian entity, presumably on the West Bank.

Begin rejected the fifth point out of hand, but promised to discuss the others with his cabinet. On the other hand it would be Begin's willingness to see Israel withdraw completely from the Sinai that would make peace with Egypt possible.

The procedural principles Vance proposed were equally important: negotiation should lead to a comprehensive Geneva Conference, with a single Arab delegation to include Palestinians, and there should be prompt adjournment of the conference into bilateral working committees to assure that the parties, not the conference, would deal with each issue, minimizing the possibility of propaganda. This last principle was to assure that each issue would not become a focus of Arab attack.

Begin seemed to agree both to Carter's points and Vance's principles, but subsequently denied he had accepted phased withdrawal on all fronts, by which of course he meant the West Bank. Upon return to Israel he sent Carter a personal message asking that Vance refrain from presenting anything with which he, Begin, had disagreed—a proposal that Carter courteously rejected. The President was standing on his determination that America would act evenhandedly, which he had to do if there was to be any progress.

Over the course of their dealings Vance would find Begin's behavior most difficult in two respects: the Israeli would seek to impose terms of confidentiality upon the administration with respect to its position on issues while reserving the right to propagandize with the American Jewish community in Israel's favor, and he would make what were thought to be iron-clad promises to delay or not continue West Bank settlements only to return to Jerusalem and go back on his promises. To be sure, the Arab governments were no better. "The more I dealt with Arab leaders," Carter had occasion to note, "the more disparity I discovered between their private assurances and their public comments . . . None of them—apart from Sadat—was willing to get in front and publicly admit a willingness to deal with Israel."[9]

As mentioned, Vance and his advisers decided to hold back the American position until each government had submitted its terms either in the form of a draft treaty or in negotiations with Vance. By this process he hoped to narrow the areas of disagreement to a point where all the parties would have a stake in attending a reconvened Geneva Conference. The United States would seek to find a negotiating partner (or partners) for Israel—which would accept Israel's right to exist, but not expect Israel to commit itself immediately to a Palestinian state on the West Bank. The unwillingness of Israel even to discuss this possibility provided Arab governments with their most determined argument for refusing to negotiate. Vance hoped that if he could get Israel to accept some form of territorial autonomy for the Palestinian people on the West Bank and Gaza, that would win support of some if not all Arab governments and neutralize the PLO. A partial breakthrough would come when Begin agreed to accept a five-year transition during which the Palestinians would receive autonomy.

In mid-August 1977, Vance undertook a second round of Middle East negotiations, visiting each capital. His assistants noticed that Arab and Israeli leaders alike were stunned by the candor with which he revealed the full terms of the other side's demands and concessions. Kissinger's style had been to hold back the full extent of concessions so he could later take credit for the increment. In the end his reputation for candor may have been as valuable for Vance as was Kissinger's reputation for cleverness.

The concession with which Vance hoped to bridge the gap between the Arab demand for a Palestinian state and Israeli rejection of the idea was a "transitional arrangement" for the West Bank and Gaza. Unfortunately, however temptingly he might bait his appeal to the PLO and the Arab countries, the PLO still demanded a state and no mention of Israel's right to exist. When word that Vance had offered to talk to the PLO found its way into the press, Begin angrily lectured him for violating a commitment. Vance got nowhere in efforts to explain that if the PLO accepted Resolution 242, that would supercede the so-called PLO Covenant that called for destruction of Israel. Throughout all this he did his utmost to avoid losing patience or making threats. But his "firm, strong streak" made Vance continue to speak his mind. In fact he was convinced that the administration ought to take the heat and push Israel harder regarding settlements on the West Bank.[10]

The key was to get the American Jewish community to see that much of what the administration proposed would be in Israel's own interest, even if Begin would not accept it. Sometimes Vance succeeded in this respect, sometimes he did not. At no time did anyone in the administration let frustration with Begin blind them to America's commitment to Israel's survival, even when the American effort for peace was under savage attack from Israel's American supporters.

The outcome of Vance's diplomacy the summer of 1977 was that Israel and Egypt each produced a draft peace treaty that Vance then showed to the other. "The very existence of these two draft treaties," the Egyptian Foreign Minister Ismail Fahmy later wrote, "was a significant development. Never before in thirty years of conflict had Israel and Egypt managed to get beyond rhetorical statements . . ."[11]

Vance then decided the time had come to call for reconvening the Geneva Conference. Over several weeks, and doubtless as part of a strategy to speed SALT, he met with Dobrynin to discuss a joint communiqué setting forth terms on which a conference would begin. Moscow publicly committed itself to seeking a settlement between Israel and the Arabs, and promised not to refer to its policy in support of an independent Palestinian state. Vance consulted Foreign Minister Moshe Dayan on release of a joint U.S.-U.S.S.R. communiqué. Dayan was not enthusiastic but seemed to offer no objection. It was released on October 1.

Thereupon everything turned downward again. The administration was shocked by the uproar both from Israel and from the Jewish community and its supporters in Congress, upon release of the joint Soviet-American communiqué looking to the Geneva Conference. Dayan may have failed to warn of Israel's sensitivity. Israel had two objections. For one, Israeli opinion was provoked by the prospect of letting the Soviet Union take part in Middle Eastern affairs. And for the other, the communiqué had referred to "legitimate rights of the Palestinian people"—a point that Vance had sought to keep vague but consistent with the purpose for which he was calling the conference, namely, to discuss a solution to the Palestinian problem. Even though the Israeli government understood that Palestinian representatives would be present as part of a single Arab delegation, and that a working group representing Israel, Egypt, Jordan, and the Palestinians would discuss the West Bank, the very mention of Palestinian rights aroused alarm among Israelis, a majority of whom now opposed any form of Palestinian state on the West Bank.

But what was Vance to have done, other than what he had proposed? It was a necessary risk. He had no illusions that the conference would be without troubles. Of plans for the conference Foreign Minister Fahmy afterward wrote:

> It is not my intention to minimize the problems which existed at this time, but one should not overestimate them either, as many analysts have done. . . . If everybody had been able to agree on an ideal basis for convening the conference, there would have been no necessity for a conference at all. [12]

Unfortunately the proposed conference received the coup de grâce from an entirely unexpected direction, one which led to Fahmy's resignation. Unknown to the Carter administration, Dayan had met in Morocco with an Egyptian foreign office representative and had said that Israel would negotiate return of the Sinai in exchange for recognition and an end to threats of war. Dayan's proposal was the condition for Sadat's dramatic decision to fly to Jerusalem in December of 1977. Whether impatience to secure the return of the Sinai and American economic backing prompted Sadat's trip, or instability and illusions of grandeur as Fahmy implies, the result was a monkey wrench in the American plan.

Although it made possible an Israeli-Egyptian negotiation that would result in the Camp David accords, it drove the other Arab states into opposition and finished off any immediate possibility of a comprehensive approach.

Everything then moved toward a meeting of only the Israelis and the Egyptians. Before giving up on the possibility of a larger meeting, however, the Carter administration made one last try, in the course of which it again raised the Palestinian issue. The latter had to be raised, for Arab states all continued to make independence for the Palestinians a condition for any negotiation. To strengthen Sadat in the course of a winter round of visits to India, Iran, Saudi Arabia, and Egypt, the President stated that parties to any final agreement had to recognize the rights of the Palestinian people. Vance and his associates worked out a nine-point West Bank–Gaza framework that he hoped would appeal to Arab moderates—this to bridge the gap between Begin's five-year, limited-self-rule plan and the need to attract the Saudis and Jordanians. The points stated were: (1) the Israeli principle of a five-year transition, during which the West Bank's inhabitants would enjoy self-rule; (2) self-rule would derive from Jordan and Egypt as well as Israel; (3) Israeli defense forces would remain, but withdraw to specified encampments; and (4) during the transition Israel, Egypt, and Jordan would negotiate Israeli withdrawal to the 1967 borders with minor modifications. The points involved terms on which the status and relation of the West Bank to Israel and Jordan would develop, an arrangement for West Bank Palestinians that Sadat could defend against the other Arab states.

Vance decided to apply pressure, and on February 16, 1978, he warned Dayan that the United States would not support Israel in pushing Sadat to a bilateral agreement with Israel that failed to deal with the West Bank and Gaza. This was a warning to Israel that it could not expect to get U.S. backing for a peace with its principal Arab threat unless it showed flexibility on the West Bank. All this to the steady musket fire between Washington and Tel Aviv about Israeli settlements on the West Bank.

To this musket fire was suddenly added an incredible round of heavy salvos. Partly to compensate Egypt for loss of the Soviet military connection, and to sustain Saudi support for Sadat and a

Saudi request for new fighters, the administration put together a package sale of jet aircraft to Egypt, Saudi Arabia, and Israel worth $4.8 billion. This included transfer to Israel under highly favorable credit terms of ninety of America's latest fighters, the F-15s and F-16s.

Concerned that Congress would see it as an attempt to circumvent its authority, Vance initially opposed the package strategy. As he anticipated, the congressional reaction was extremely adverse, Senator Frank Church, Chairman of the Foreign Relations Committee, called the package "improper and unintended by the law"—referring to the Nelson-Bingham Act reserving to Congress the opportunity for evaluation and modification of military sales. In the ensuing controversy the Senate majority leader, Robert Byrd, proposed and the White House agreed that it would unlock the package in return for assurance that the Senate would vote for the Saudi and Egyptian sales. "The next morning Carter sent Byrd a draft of a letter Vance would send to Senator Church 'unlocking the package,' " while preserving the administration's option "to review the action taken by the Congress. In the Senator's opinion 'it was enough to unruffle feathers' " and avoid a split with Congress.

The hearings demanded all of Vance's skill and patience and were long and arduous. The staff report prepared by the Foreign Relations Committee favored sale to the Saudis, as did the House International Relations Committee, although not the majority. Senator Abraham Ribicoff, a prominent Jewish member of the committee, endorsed the sale, providing cover for those favoring the package. In the end the administration accepted a proposal that Israel receive an additional twenty F-15s to make a fairer balance, and Vance met with members of both committees where he announced acceptance of the concessions. The compromise permitted the passage of Middle East arms sales on terms that strengthened the administration's policy.

Here again the challenge to Israel's privileged position drew fire both from Tel Aviv and Israel's American supporters. Again Vance was convinced the deal was even-handed and essential to America's position, and to Saudi support for Egyptian positions vis-à-vis the "rejectionist" front. Much of his time was spent on the Hill testifying before hostile committees with what most commentators considered persuasiveness under difficult circumstances.

The fact that for the first time an American administration was willing to sell arms to Arab regimes of a quantity and sophistication equal to those being sold to Israel came as a shock to both Israelis and American Jews. As a private observer remarked upon return from the Middle East,

One is struck, in discussions with Israeli leaders, by the refusal of many to acknowledge the new realities in the Middle East. The image is of an either/or relationship, a zero-sum game with little willingness to accept the creation of a new Arab-American relationship side-by-side with the continuing U.S.-Israeli one. To the extent that this new relationship's existence is acknowledged, it is seen as the result of momentary factors such as the public relations success of Sadat's peace initiative, or the alleged tilt of the Carter administration toward the Arabs. Rarely does one hear the view that a closer American relationship with the Arabs may facilitate the difficult task of negotiating peace.[13]

About this time Israeli public opinion polls showed a majority of Israelis in favor of Palestinian autonomy on the West Bank, provided there were guarantees. Unfortunately Palestinian terrorists operating out of Lebanon launched a murderous attack from the sea, under cover of darkness, kidnapping and killing Israeli civilians. Opinion again swung behind Begin, who ordered a massive counterstrike into Lebanon south of the Litani River. Thus began the Israeli relationship with Christian militiamen in southern Lebanon under Major Haddad. The terrorist attack greatly strengthened Begin's hand.

When the Israeli prime minister arrived in Washington in March 1978, the encounter from the outset was confrontational. The Israeli government had always argued that if any Arab state was willing to negotiate, it would be reasonable. As Carter pointed out to Begin, Sadat was not insisting either on withdrawal to the 1967 borders on the West Bank or upon an independent Palestinian state on the West Bank and in Gaza. All that he asked of the Israeli government was to agree to a transitional regime under Israeli military safeguards, at the end of which autonomy for the Palestinians would be considered. Under pressure from Carter, Begin agreed to consider Vance's suggestion of an agreement between Israel and Jordan, providing for a self-governing Palestinian authority. Vance determined to find some way to negotiate terms for the area during the transition. Dayan hoped that if Vance could get the Egyptians to agree to leave settlement of the issue of the West Bank's government to the future rather than tackling it at the beginning of the transition period, there could be a breakthrough. Vance was skeptical but willing to try. If the West Bank issue could not be settled at the beginning of the transition, Vance recognized that there had to be arrangements for negotiating during the transition. He asked that Dayan secure Israeli agreement to two questions: "Would Israel agree that at the end of the five years a decision would be made on the final status and sovereignty of the territories; and would Israel outline the mechanism by which this change would be negotiated?"[14] When the Israeli reply proved inadequate, Vance said so. That and the military package underlined the administration's determination not to be flummoxed. With some indication from Sadat that he would not be averse to Israeli troops remaining on the West Bank during the transition, Vance was ready to bring the parties together again.[15]

Having gotten Begin to go about as far as was possible, Vance turned to the problem created by Sadat's impulsive decision to break off negotiation following Begin's alleged insult to the new Egyptian foreign minister, Muhammed Kamel, in the course of a dinner address. Here is where Carter's friendship with Sadat paid off. Despite frustration with Begin and threats from Arab states, Sadat showed himself willing to accommodate his friend "Jimmy." One must not depict Sadat's courage in too sentimental a light. He had a stake in regaining the Sinai and generally in peace with Israel. Sadat agreed to have his foreign minister and Begin's meet Vance in London on July 11. For security reasons, the meetings were moved to Leeds Castle in Kent, where Vance and his wife, who had accompanied him, succeeded in breaking the social if not diplomatic ice. In face-to-face discussion Dayan and Kamel reknit the threads of negotiation that had been severed the previous January.

Even more significant was Dayan's decision to risk Begin's displeasure by handing Vance a note expressing opinion that Israel would be prepared to discuss the key issue of sovereignty over the West Bank and Gaza after five years of autonomy. "As Dayan must have expected, Begin was infuriated by both his idea and his insubordination."[16] Nevertheless to Dayan's astonishment, "Begin proposed that the Cabinet endorse his memorandum to Vance and bring it to the Knesset for approval, which it won by sixty-four votes to thirty-two."[17] Vance had won a critical concession because the Dayan memorandum became an official document representing Israel's position and opened the way to Camp David.

The Leeds Conference of Vance and the Israeli and Egyptian foreign ministers convinced the American Secretary of State that the time was right to present his country's Middle East proposals and enter the picture not just as a mediator but as a full partner. Not everything proved immediately easy. Despite some Israeli flexibility on the West Bank, the Israeli cabinet's rejection of Sadat's request for return of the Sinai towns of El Arish and Mt. Sinai touched off yet another round of acrimony. Again Vance had to leave on a Middle East "rescue mission." This time he carried the President's invitation to Begin and Sadat to meet at Camp David in September.

The Camp David invitation to the two Middle East disputants came at the right moment, with Begin under pressure from within Israel and Sadat anxious to show some gain. Begin argued that the U.S. should continue the intermediary role and not offer proposals. Vance believed that time was over. He and his associates had reached a point where they would place the President's prestige in the balance for peace.

# CHAPTER EIGHT

# *World Order Agenda*

SALT II and Middle East negotiations, issues discussed in previous chapters, were a continuation of policies under Nixon and Kissinger. But the Carter administration had dedicated itself to a new relationship. It determined to emphasize the qualities for which America stood, in promoting a new world order based on human rights and self-determination, international law and the rights of others. Carter gave this mood an almost evangelistic expression in his 1977 Notre Dame commencement speech:

> Our policy is based on a historical vision of America's role. Our policy is derived from a large view of global change. Our policy is rooted in our moral values, which never change. Our policy is reinforced by our material wealth and by our military power. Our policy is designed to serve mankind.

Under Nixon and Kissinger most issues had been subordinate to the Soviet relationship and America's primacy within the world system. National self-determination in southern Africa and the basic questions in the Middle East were hardly considerations because they had little to contribute to maintaining the status quo. Human rights was given hardly any attention.[1] Nor was Latin America.[2] Carter determined to change such priorities.

Vance shared many of Carter's ideals, albeit with a more modest emphasis, because he beheld more complexities. He believed the world was in vast social and political change, which neither superpower could control. He believed it was in America's interest to support movements for change, or at least not categorically oppose them. He was confident that change would not be detrimental to America's strategic and long-run interest and that in many instances America could apply its resources in a way that would turn a deteriorating situation into a stable one. It was his determination to adapt American policy to realities that marked Vance's approach, not lack of will in containing the Soviet Union. What was distinctive about Vance's approach was belief that America's strength gave it the power to contain Soviet influence short of confrontation.

He believed implicitly that problems and conflicts were resolvable provided sufficient understanding was applied. He believed that to be effective in foreign policy the U.S. had to demonstrate understanding and respect for other people and states. Ideals were not sufficient unless attended by conduct.

This did not mean he ignored the clashes inherent in the state system, but he believed that America should live up to its ideals and act out of respect for other governments.[3] Vance attempted to understand Soviet perceptions of reality, instead of automatically assigning evil intentions.[4] He felt that the new administration should bring "a new sensitivity, awareness and priority" to relations between America and the Third World, an "unwavering stand in favor of the rights of free men without unrealistically inserting itself into the internal operations of other governments."[5] It would not "try to do everything at once or solve all the world's problems."[6]

The administration especially wanted to end any patronizing relation with Latin American neighbors, including U.S. sovereignty over the Panama Canal Zone (the last remnant of formal colonialism in the Western Hemisphere); advance human rights; and curb transfer of nuclear technology for military purposes. In seeking world order it was necessary to start somewhere, and so Vance decided to begin with the Panama Canal Zone.

The possibility of relinquishing American sovereignty over the Canal Zone had been under negotiation between Panama and the United States for a decade. As in the Vladivostok accords, a tentative agreement with Panama, worked out by Kissinger, provided for the return of the zone to Panama within a specific time period, during which the United States would retain the right to operate and defend the canal. The proposed treaty had been sidetracked by domestic political considerations. Public opinion, spearheaded by Governor Reagan of California, favored preserving the status quo by a margin of nearly 80 percent to less than 10 percent.

In anticipation of the administration's determination to negotiate, Vance had asked Sol Linowitz, former ambassador to the Organization of American States and ex-chairman of the Xerox Corporation, to serve with Ellsworth Bunker.[7] Settlement of the canal issue would show Latin Americans that the administration was serious about achieving a less patronizing relationship. Not content with moving on the canal, Carter initiated a plan for renewing diplomatic relations with Cuba and toward improving relations with Jamaica and Guyana.

Having appointed negotiators, Vance believed in giving them latitude to explore without being subject to day-to-day direction. The issue was how to retain the American right to defend the canal without infringing on the proposed Panamanian sovereignty.

If Vance and Carter assumed that such a treaty could be negotiated quickly, perhaps as a preliminary to SALT II and normalization of relations with China, they were wrong. Vance's role for much of the negotiation was limited to working with the President and Brzezinski, so as to give Linowitz and Bunker guidance and dampen the campaign by the Panamanian negotiator, Romulo Escobar, to eliminate the U.S. role in protecting the canal and to extract a huge sum, estimated at over $3 billion, as compensation for sixty years of U.S. exploitation. Congressmen were kept abreast of the negotiation by Bunker and Linowitz.

A brilliant stroke in negotiation was the negotiators' suggestion to negotiate two treaties—one of indefinite duration giving the United States the right to defend the canal, and a second transferring the canal to Panama, the transfer to be completed by the year 2000. By separating the issues, the negotiators hoped that the U.S. right to defend the canal would prove acceptable.

Vance's role emerged with the signing of the treaties on September 7, 1977, and their submission to the Senate. Opposition to having the Canal Zone revert to Panama had declined. Conceding to Panama something as symbolic of American power as the canal was bound to provoke controversy, however. Its construction had exemplified a heroic era in American life; in an age of superpower rivalry the canal appeared necessary to America's security. That it was no longer wide enough to take carriers and that the United States had fleets in both oceans was not convincing to critics who believed that America's lifeline was the Canal Zone. The treaties hence raised an issue between the Carter administration and such critics as Governor Reagan of California, who argued that to give up the canal would be one more example of the decline of American power that had begun with abandonment of South Vietnam.

From September 26, 1977, when he defended the treaties before the Foreign Relations Committee, until April 18, 1978, Vance was involved in efforts—first public, then in negotiation with the Senate—to permit the administration to muster enough votes for consent. To educate the public, the administration invoked the support of Kissinger, Ford, the joint chiefs, and every other possible authority. The opposition countered with a massive campaign mounted by conservatives, hawks, and right-wingers in general. The Senate gradually became the focus of both efforts. In the winter and spring of 1977–1978, no less than thirty senators and their staffs made visits to Panama and met the Panamanian leader, General Omar Torrijos. Scores of amendments and reservations were proposed, which were at length eliminated through cooperation between Senate leaders and the President. Vance wisely turned management of the treaties over to Undersecretary Christopher, who developed close relations with both the Republican minority leader, Senator Howard Baker, and the majority leader, Byrd. The first treaty, providing for Panamanian control over the canal and the zone, passed the Senate by vote of 68 to 32 (one vote more than necessary) on March 16, 1978.

The most determined effort in the Senate to kill the Panamanian agreement was Senator Dennis DeConcini's proposed amendment to the neutrality treaty, but the administration managed to surmount it. The gist of the amendment was that the United States and Panama "shall each independently have the right to take such steps as it deems necessary . . . including the use of military force in Panama, to reopen the canal or restore the operation of the canal as the case may be." To get around this, a wording had to be found that assured the Senate of American right to maintain the neutrality of the canal and at the same time not appear to Panamanians to give the United States the right of intervention. In an inspired move, the Panamanians proposed mediation by former Assistant Secretary of State for inter-American affairs William D. Rogers, at that time practicing law with Arnold and Porter. Rogers, who had been advising Baker, accepted with the provision that he work with the Senate leadership, with Christopher, and with Ambassador William J. Jorden and his Panamanian counterpart Gabriel Lewis Galindo. On April 7, with the vote set for the 17th, the White House agreed to stand aside. Christopher and the Senate leaders in consultation with the Panamanians negotiated a wording to the second treaty that met Panama's objection to the DeConcini amendment and also satisfied the Senate leadership. Retaining the principle of the canal's neutrality, it restated the U.S. commitment to nonintervention. Its core was a Panamanian-drafted clause that nothing in either treaty would give the United States "right of intervention in the internal affairs of the Republic of Panama or interference with its political independence or sovereign integrity." The Senate leadership's resolution conspicuously failed to reiterate DeConcini's phrase guaranteeing the United States the right to employ "military force in the Republic of Panama" to keep the canal open. With bipartisan support on the part of the Senate leaders, the neutrality treaty, guaranteeing to all nations the right to use the canal in peace and war but implying a residual right to the United States to take action if Panama failed, passed on April 18, again by one vote, 68 to 32.

While the treaties drew intense criticism domestically, they proved highly acceptable to the Panamanian people and demonstrated the wisdom of the nonintervention pledge for winning General Torrijos's support. Two years later when the administration was desperately seeking a refuge for the Shah of Iran and Mexico would no longer accept him, Torrijos graciously agreed.

The administration had been unrealistic in expecting that so controversial a treaty could be negotiated during its first year. But to say that a great deal of political capital had been expended overlooks the fact that the alternatives would have been grim. At considerable political cost, President Carter had concluded a necessary undertaking that none of his predecessors was willing to risk.[8] He had eliminated the most obvious symbol of American colonialism in the region.

Among other items on the administration's world order agenda, nothing more symbolized its attempt to restore principle than its human rights policy. Carter often defined it in absolute terms. On September 8, 1976, during an appearance before the B'nai B'rith, he had declared:

> We cannot look away when a government tortures its people, or jails them for their beliefs or denies minorities fair treatment. . . . We should begin by having it understood that if any nation . . . deprives its own people of basic human rights, that fact will shape our own people's attitudes toward that nation's government.

No doubt the favorable reception for human rights during the campaign gave Carter incentive to continue. He believed in human rights, or otherwise it would not have continued to figure in his presidency even after it had become an object of controversy. By his inauguration no one was startled to hear him assert that "our commitment to human rights must be absolute. Our moral sense dictates a clearcut preference for those societies which share with us an abiding respect for human rights."[9] Two years later he still insisted upon his commitment, in the strongest terms:

> As long as I am President, the government of the United States will continue throughout the world to enhance human rights. Our human rights policy is not a decoration. It is not something we have adopted to polish up our image abroad, or to put a fresh coat of paint on the discredited policies of the past. Human rights is the soul of our foreign policy.[10]

Human rights was one of the flags under which Carter determined to sail the ship of state. It was emblematic of his hope to create a consensus around the proposition that the United States had a foreign policy as good as the American people. The public had been shocked by revelations of complicity with regimes guilty of torture and murder. Carter believed that if he could make human rights a principle of policy, Americans would regain faith in internationalism.

Given the President's views, whoever was Secretary of State

would have been bound to uphold them. Fortunately Vance shared Carter's commitment, but with more tempered expectation. His commitment sprang from a horror over what was being done—most victims were guilty of nothing more than protest against exploitation—and from a sense of shame that the United States should appear not only insensitive to this suffering but indulgent toward repressive regimes.

Vance was also convinced that it was in America's interest to encourage allied or dependent governments to base their rule on something more legitimate than murder and torture. Changes were occurring. Even so repressive a state as the Soviet Union had modified its behavior toward dissidents. With transformation occurring in many Third World countries, time appeared to be running out for many oligarchies and dictatorships. If the danger from Marxist revolution was to be reduced, governments would need to be responsive to their citizens. Nothing could serve the United States both in competition with the Soviet Union and in her aspiration for a civilized world better than an emphasis upon human rights. The U.S. had all too often let itself be used as an accomplice to repression, even when there was no security interest. Vance determined to end that.

Reflecting the President's wishes, Vance appeared before the Senate Appropriations Committee's subcommittee on foreign operations to announce that the administration planned to reduce aid to Argentina, Ethiopia, and Uruguay. The list expanded to include other countries, one of which—Brazil—thereupon abrogated its military aid agreement with the United States. Vance indicated that while rights violations would receive attention, he would incorporate them into policy on a country-by-country basis. "In each case we must balance a political concern for human rights considerations against economic or security goals."[11]

Vance refined the role of human rights in a speech at the University of Georgia in April 1977. He and his associates had had time to examine the issue and the speech expressed a restraint that previous human rights declarations had not had. "In pursuing a human rights policy," he said, "we must always keep in mind the limits of our power and wisdom. A sure formula for defeat of our goals would be a rigid, hubristic attempt to impose our values on others. A doctrinaire plan of action would be as damaging as indifference." He indicated that the United States envisioned three categories of rights. First was violation of the physical integrity of individuals "by torture, or cruel, inhuman or degrading treatment or punishment, or prolonged detention without charges." Second, socioeconomic rights such as food, shelter, health care, education. Until then these latter rights had not figured in policy, even though foreign aid was devoted to them. Vance and his associates were taking a leaf from Marxist and Third World declarations that give pride of place to a material base for life.[12] Third, he accorded importance to civil and political rights. This provided Americans with a hierarchy to evaluate a country's rights record.

Vance's determination not to evade the human rights issue was never more apparent than at the seventh general assembly of the Organization of American States in June 1977, when he offered a rebuttal to the contention that human rights abuses were an unfortunate but necessary byproduct of the war against terror. In contrast to Kissinger, he rejected the efficacy of combating terror with terror.

> If terrorism and violence in the name of dissent cannot be condoned, neither can violence that is officially sanctioned. The surest way to defeat terrorism is to promote justice in our societies—legal, social and economic justice. Justice that is summary undermines the future it seeks to promote. It produces only more violence, more victims, and more terrorism.

The United States also cosponsored (and helped obtain votes for) a resolution that stated that no circumstances "justify torture, summary executions or prolonged detention without trial contrary to law."[14]

A second action through which the administration signaled the importance of human rights was its decision to upgrade the area in the Department of State by creating a Bureau of Human Rights and Humanitarian Affairs and, perhaps equally important, appointing Patricia Derian to head it. A civil rights activist, a founder of the Mississippi Civil Liberties Union, an organizer of the biracial Loyalist Mississippi Democratic Party that unsuccessfully challenged the all-white delegation at the 1968 Democratic Party convention, Ms. Derian was a person of "unusually strong will . . . who was not intimidated by established bureaucratic procedures," and who did not hesitate gracefully but firmly to challenge such dictators as crossed her path, including their responsibilities for torture and murder.[15]

Vance also assigned Christopher to head an interagency group on human rights and foreign assistance—to approve, delay, limit, or deny any proposed project on the basis of the recipient country's rights record. As one observer remarked,

> Opponents within the bureaucracy of the new human rights emphasis might be able to box in or do end runs around the efforts of Assistant Secretary of State Derian and her newly enlarged Office of Human Rights and Humanitarian Affairs, but not the Secretary of State's most trusted second in command presiding over a powerful interagency group with members from the Departments of Defense, Treasury, Commerce, Labor, Agriculture, and the National Security Council. Decisions of the Christopher group were tantamount to an executive order, and were backed up by the appropriate White House and Cabinet-level endorsements when required.

Before Carter became President and Vance Secretary of State, executive support for human rights had been virtually nil and emphasis had been on "quiet diplomacy," a euphemism for no diplomacy. The prevailing view was that if the United States pressed human rights violators, the governments would not only be insulted but reject interference. To the Nixon and Ford administrations, quiet diplomacy on behalf of human rights involved only the most circumspect of protests.

Vance changed that. Terence A. Todman, a career diplomat, had been the administration's appointee as head of the Bureau of Inter-American Affairs. He had opposed the use of public diplomacy and aid cut-offs to protest human rights in Latin America. Upon completion of a trip to Chile in October 1977, he had expressed satisfaction with events, and in February 1978 during a speech, he listed ten tactical mistakes in promoting human rights. "Among these were the practice of 'condemning an entire government for every negative act by one of its officials.' "[17] This was the excuse frequently given by dictators. Todman's appointment, following this speech, to the ambassadorship to Spain was Vance's and Carter's signal that they would continue to pursue human rights vigorously.

A common complaint about the Department of State was "clientelism"—that the Department was not responsive to the wishes of the President but preferred to maintain independent relations with foreign governments. This was not true in the case of human rights, which were pursued to the utmost diplomatic tolerance, bilaterally and multilaterally.[18] Wherever it was possible to demonstrate support for human rights, Vance approved. Instead of holding back ratifying United Nations human rights conventions, the U.S. not only did so but took the lead in international forums for strengthening legal and moral norms protecting human rights. Carter signed the two 1966 U.N. conventions on human rights and submitted them to the Senate.[19]

Vance honored congressional legislation directing the State Department to submit annual reports on human rights in countries receiving security or economic assistance. Reports prepared by the State Department not only went to Congress, but each embassy gave them to its host government and often discussed them. Responses appear to have varied. Reports had a mixed reception in Latin American countries and little effect upon relations elsewhere. But the campaign seemed to move some governments to modify their behavior.

Nor did Vance interfere with Assistant Secretary Derian's raising issues directly with foreign officials. Eschewing "quiet diplomacy," which was so quiet it was rarely heard, the State Department was "willing to push the issue beyond the bounds of normal diplomatic intercourse." Conversation with leaders of repressive governments was frank and extremely tense. It was not easy to talk about torture and murder.[20]

On a case-by-case basis Vance drew the line at human rights sanctions against countries essential to American security, such as South Korea, the Philippines, and Iran. Where economic aid was deemed vital for humanitarian or development purposes, he also determined that human rights should not be the only standard.

Application to Russia was a perplexing problem, which he resolved in favor of preserving SALT II. Soviet treatment of dissidents was soft-pedaled without being neglected.[21] Over Brzezinski's opposition Vance prevailed upon Carter to soften the U.S. position at the autumn 1977 sessions of the Belgrade review conference on the Helsinki Accords (the 1975 East-West agreement on human rights cooperation in Europe), in part out of respect for our allies' desire to protect what little progress the accords had achieved and out of desire not to worsen Soviet-American relations.[22]

Elsewhere he applied the standard with rigor. He barred military and economic assistance to the Central African Empire, Chile, Mozambique, Angola, and Vietnam. Where possible he steered human rights into multilateral channels. "In the Nicaraguan case, for example, the United States was careful to place its policies within the framework of the OAS. Diplomatic efforts to remove Somoza were by collective mediation, and only when that failed were unilateral steps taken to terminate aid."[23]

Vance was less willing and hence less successful in following congressional instructions to consider human rights in financial decisions of the multinational lending agencies. Nevertheless the U.S. abstained on some proposals before the World Bank and International Monetary Fund and voted "no" on others on human rights grounds. Inasmuch as development aid advanced human rights in the economic, health and education fields, Vance was reluctant to oppose such aid except in egregious cases.

Once again the charge against the administration was that policy on human rights lacked "a strategic conception of how to link ethics and expediency." In fact no strategic concept could have linked ethics and expediency in human rights diplomacy.

How much good did the human rights policy do? Vance never made any soaring claim. Like so many aspects of policy, its effects were shrouded in ambiguity. It did not provide the basis for the new policy consensus hoped for by President Carter. In fact, it probably added to domestic conflict over policy. Conservatives complained that the focus on human rights underestimated the totalitarian threat from communism at the expense of our allies. Vance argued that not only was defense of human rights a moral ideal that had relevance to America's search for world order, but support for regimes that violated human rights carried grave risks of indulging them in practices inimical to their own survival. On the other side, the administration's performance compared to the standards proclaimed early on by Carter—not Vance's more realistic refinements—enabled critics to vilify the administration for hypocrisy.

Surely a world order agenda was easier to state than to carry out, and yet in retrospect the Carter administration did its best to settle the Panama Canal Zone issue, and that of human rights. Likewise it sought to limit nuclear proliferation by preventing the sale of nuclear reactors and reprocessing plants by Germany and France to Third World states like South Korea, Brazil, and Pakistan. There was a touch of irony in the fact that an administration desiring to improve relations with Western Europe as well as guard against proliferation should have had to battle two of its most important allies over the issue.

The Ford administration had seen that the sale of nuclear reprocessing plants by France and Germany made possible the conversion of spent nuclear fuel rods into weapons-grade plutonium. In breeder reactors, plutonium afforded an almost inexhaustible source of energy, but an almost unparalleled source of danger if terrorists or unstable Third World governments diverted it to weapons. Carter had learned of the problem during seminars of the Trilateral Commission. As the leading nuclear power and nuclear fuel supplier, the United States, he felt, should do something. The only problem was that West Germany, France, and Japan had committed themselves to nuclear reprocessing and the sale of such plants. Breeder technology, its foreign advocates argued, was cheaper, and it also reduced dependence on U.S. nuclear supplies. Both the allies and Third World countries were bound to resist any new set of U.S. controls in reprocessing spent nuclear fuel or sale of reprocessing plants or development of breeder reactors.

Within the administration, pressure for action against transfer of nuclear technology came from the NSC staff, which shared Carter's almost apocalyptic concern about proliferation. The position of what one writer described as the "purists" was to "strive mightily in a moral cause." The purists, this writer said, were more than presidential advisers: "They were the public manifestation of his superego."[24] On the other side were domestic supporters of nuclear energy, both in the bureaucracy and in private industry, who opposed closing the nuclear reprocessing project at Barnwell, South

Carolina, and foregoing the complex and costly breeder project scheduled for start-up at the Clinch River site in Tennessee.

The initial administration move had unhappy results. Inspired by knowledge that West Germany was about to approve export licenses for sale of sensitive reprocessing technology to Brazil, the White House dispatched Vice President Mondale to Bonn. But Chancellor Schmidt was in no mood to be accommodating, and to the applause of German political circles he rebuffed Mondale. The Brazilian response to the attempt to block the deal was even more curt. Brazil's quest for great power status had made it sensitive to slights by its North American neighbor, and relations had become strained because of Washington's criticism of the regime's human rights record.[25]

Faced with such opposition, the President adopted a two-fold policy. In a statement on April 7, 1977, he expressed hope that other governments would "join with us in trying to have some further world-wide understanding of the extreme threat of the further proliferation of nuclear explosive capability." He proposed that nuclear suppliers carry out an international fuel-cycle evaluation to determine the dangers from unguarded reprocessing. His second course was drastic unilateral action to convince Europeans of the danger from plutonium production and demonstrate that the United States was willing to accompany words with action. He ordered the Barnwell operation shut down and the Clinch River breeder reactor put on hold.

The Carter administration's policy against proliferation stalled at this point and, alas, not much more came from it. Domestic critics rose up in wrath. Foreign critics got the message about administration displeasure, but did little to change their behavior. Perhaps proliferation was too complicated a proposition for the people of the world, or the American public and the publics of West European nations. Its concrete manifestations, in possible loss of orders for expensive equipment, for the apparent giving up of new technology, seemed like unnecessary sacrifices, especialy when so drawn by critics who had much to lose if orders were abandoned. Feelings against the United States, raised up for whatever reasons, could always be focused on some matter of the moment, such as the Americans' anti-proliferation campaign—any superpower, such as the United States, was subject to almost instant hostilities that might well have little to do with the issue of the moment. Good policies, such as the Carter effort to stop proliferation, could come to nothing in the face of this kind of opposition. A world order agenda thus was easy to announce and devilishly difficult to carry through.

# CHAPTER NINE

# *NATO*

Among the aspirations with which the Carter administration entered office was the desire to strengthen America's political and military ties with the European allies. Vance therefore gave much attention to NATO. His difficulties, and there were many, stemmed from the economic policies of the United States under preceding administrations, which had irritated the NATO allies and persuaded them that only with more responsible policies should the American government expect more European cooperation.

The nations of Europe indeed had good reason to be irritated with the United States. For almost a decade the Americans had endeavored to maintain world hegemony and at the same time greatly expand social spending at home, despite declining economic power relative to other capitalist economies. The Johnson and Nixon administrations had passed much of the cost to America's allies, forcing them to hold onto dollars generated by U.S. spending abroad. They neglected inflationary pressures generated by deficit spending and monetary expansion at home. When the Organization of Petroleum Exporting Nations hiked prices of oil in 1973, the result was not greater economic discipline in the United States, but only increased inflation.[1]

Carter tried to repeat his predecessors' expedient of exporting the United States's economic problems. Rather than cut back the American economy to make it more competitive, he would try to persuade West Germany, France, and Japan to expand their economies so as to increase demand for U.S. goods. Other nations that could afford a trade deficit should expand along with the United States.

This policy called upon allies to serve as "locomotives" for the American economy, and the locomotive theory seemed outrageous to such Europeans as West German Chancellor Schmidt. A Social Democrat, he had just put the West German economy through the wringer of recession to squeeze out the OPEC oil price hikes. He had no intention of letting the West German economy absorb U.S. inflation. The locomotive argument and its abrupt rejection contributed to the ever-more awkward relationship that developed between Carter and Schmidt, who eventually wrote off the American president as a lightweight. Leaders of other countries felt likewise, even if they did not make Schmidt's personal appraisal. They were no longer willing to knuckle under to American economic practices detrimental to them. Not only was there increasing resistance to America's "economic indiscipline," but the decline in America's geopolitical power was making it more difficult for the United States to impose its policies. In addition, because détente had reduced East-West tensions, Europeans no longer felt compelled to subordinate their economic interests to those of the U.S.

The Carter administration came into office nonetheless determined to upgrade NATO. At the May 1977 meeting of NATO heads of government, an agreement stipulated that each member state should increase defense spending by 3 percent per year above inflation.

Although NATO's nuclear force capabilities were up for review, they did not have priority because of the Defense Department's recent buildup of American nuclear forces attached to NATO. Prior to Carter's taking office, the United States had quietly increased the submarine-launched ballistic missiles (SLBMs) at disposal of the NATO commander to five Polaris submarines with 400 Poseidon warheads capable of attacking targets in Russia. In 1977, F-111 long-range fighter bombers stationed in Britain and capable of all-weather penetration of the Soviet Union were increased from 80 to 164. Quite apart from several thousand tactical nuclear warheads, NATO possessed this additional 500 to 600 intermediate to long-range theater weapons capable of striking Soviet targets.

The American problem with NATO hence was complicated from

the outset: a complex of European irritation and of fear by European governments that their security interests might be sacrificed to a Soviet-American strategic agreement.

At this juncture the European allies began to worry that the United States would reduce its nuclear backing of NATO. European defense planners feared that the increase in American nuclear strength in NATO might not offset any substitution by the Soviet Union of more advanced missiles in place of its aging SS-4s and SS-5s. Moreover, the European governments, the West German in particular, feared that the United States would bargain away its right to deploy cruise missiles and other theater nuclear weapons in exchange for a strategic arms limitation agreement, just when deployment of SS-20s appeared likely to upset Europe's nuclear balance.

The Soviet Union had every right to argue that the West already possessed forward-based systems capable of reaching Warsaw Pact nations and that since the cruise missile could reach the Soviet Union from bases in Europe it ought to be treated as a strategic weapon and be included in the aggregate ceilings under SALT. The Kremlin had contended all along that the American forward-based systems in Europe should be part of any strategic arms limitation agreement, since the Soviets had no comparable systems in the same proximity to the United States. But the fact that the United States was negotiating a treaty that codified strategic parity between the two superpowers heightened concern in Europe that Washington might not be willing—now that it no longer enjoyed strategic nuclear superiority—to risk destruction of its homeland to ensure the defense of Western Europe. It was in this context, largely psychological, that the issue of whether the United States would match the Soviet buildup of SS-20s with deployment of land-based cruise missiles assumed importance.

As Secretary of State, Vance had both to advance U.S. interest in a strategic arms limitation agreement, by getting around Soviet objections to deployment of long-range theater nuclear weapons in Europe, and at the same time reassure NATO governments that they would not be left at a political or military disadvantage in light of a new generation of Soviet nuclear weapons for the European theater. The SS-20 did not change Europe's vulnerability to nuclear weapons from the Soviet Union. And yet NATO as of 1977 had no comparable capability. For those who worried about political implications, the SS-20 appeared to require some response.

There was a third awkwardness for an American negotiator. The credibility of the U.S. commitment to defend Europe even at risk of nuclear destruction to itself was coming to the fore at a time when European governments were under increasing public pressure to minimize the danger of nuclear war. Carter and Vance were the first President and Secretary of State to confront the contradiction between Europe's demand for an ever-more iron-clad assurance of an American nuclear guarantee and the demand that the Soviet-American rivalry not heighten the risk of nuclear confrontation.

The issue on which the matter turned in SALT II was the Soviet demand for a nontransfer provision to tie American hands with respect to cruise missiles in Europe, by requiring the parties "not to transfer strategic offensive weapons to other states, and not to assist in their development."[2] Because cruise missiles were under development, and not likely to be operational for three or four years, Vance felt nothing would be lost in an agreement to hold off deployment. To meet the European concern he secured from Gromyko an understanding that while the interim agreement or protocol to the SALT II treaty would prohibit deployment of land- or sea-based cruise missiles for three years, it did not prevent future transfers, should no agreement on limiting Soviet long-range theater nuclear weapons have been reached.

In keeping with its engagement to consult with the allies on NATO-related aspects of SALT, and not just inform them, as had been the practice under previous administrations, Vance also determined that no SALT decision of importance to European security would be taken without consultation. This arrangement he put into effect immediately.[3]

Tension remained. Vance did not alleviate Europe's suspicion of being "stalled while the United States gained time to trade away cruise missiles in SALT II,"[4] despite his effort to convince the NATO allies that nothing vital was being bargained away by a three-year moratorium on transfer of such missiles. It might have been overcome without public controversy had Cancellor Schmidt not decided to make it the issue of an October 1977 address to the London-based International Institute of Strategic Studies. Schmidt's leadership of a resurgent Germany led him to an exaggerated sense of self-importance. Had he not set out to create an éclat in European strategy circles, the problem of the three-year moratorium on cruise missiles for the theater nuclear balance in Europe might have been minimized.

One might have thought the presence of 300,000 U.S. troops in West Germany under a unified command and equipped to fight a conventional or nuclear war would by any canon of logic constitute a warrant against Soviet aggression. Whatever psychological advantage the Soviet Union might gain from deployment of SS-20s was offset by the presence of U.S. tactical and theater nuclear forces. Nevertheless, Schmidt now chose to raise doubt. He declared that SALT

> codifies the nuclear strategic balance between the Soviet Union and the United States . . . SALT neutralizes their strategic nuclear capabilities. In Europe this magnifies the significance of the disparities between East and West in nuclear tactical and conventional weapons. . . . No one can deny that the principle of parity is a sensible one. However . . . it must apply to all categories of weapons. Neither side can agree to diminish its security unilaterally . . . we in Europe must be particularly careful to ensure that these negotiations do not neglect the components of NATO's deterrence strategy . . . strategic arms limitations confined to the United States and the Soviet Union will inevitably impair the security of the West European members of the alliance vis-à-vis Soviet military superiority in Europe.

The logic of his analysis was entirely hypothetical. As Brzezinski, Kissinger, and others had occasion to observe, there had never been a Euro-strategic balance. Nevertheless, to have the West German chancellor raise doubt publicly over an issue to which the Soviets were sensitive and that challenged détente vastly complicated Vance's effort to manage both SALT negotiations and NATO relations.

And the tension produced a special problem. Schmidt also had mentioned the need to pursue arms control of theater nuclear weapons, precisely what Vance was aiming for with the option to deploy land- and sea-launched cruise missiles if, within the three-year life of SALT II, limits upon Soviet SS-20s had not been agreed to. At this point, however, the chancellor's London speech played into the hands of strategic analysts in the Pentagon, committed to production and deployment of cruise missiles on a large scale. They viewed the cruise missile not as a bargaining chip with which to limit Soviet SS-20s, but as a weapon to be deployed for its intrinsic advantage. Powerful organizational and service forces had been gathering behind the cruise missile, and Vance would now have to reckon with the Pentagon's urge to see an across-the-board buildup of nuclear weapons. Schmidt's speech seemed to foreclose whatever hope Vance may have had that issues raised by deployment of the SS-20 might be handled without resort to the cruise missile.

Vance made no attempt to challenge such European premises or conclusions and instead agreed that the High Level Group of NATO defense officials under chairmanship of Assistant Secretary of Defense David McGiffert should review NATO's long-range theater nuclear weapons. Its deliberations, running ahead of Vance's timetable, led to agreement in principle that NATO should upgrade its theater nuclear capabilities to strike targets in the Soviet Union. This was the kind of portentous recommendation that a small group of military planners free of responsibility could take without concern for political consequences.

Meanwhile discussion about the so-called neutron bomb was producing much confusion among American and European leaders and their peoples. The neutron bomb's beginnings were simple enough. The Pentagon had determined that its theater nuclear weapons in Europe possessed a high fission-fusion ratio that "upon detonation would probably produce high levels of long-term radioactivity, blast, and fallout . . . and were too powerful to use in a 'discriminate' way against enemy military forces."[6] To clean up NATO's nuclear warheads the Pentagon had ordered development of the "enhanced radiation warhead" (ERW), which would decimate enemy forces without so much radiation.[7] Development of this weapon—known as the neutron bomb—was first noticed by Walter Pincus of the *Washington Post* in June 1977 and touched off an emotional debate, principally over whether its character as an antipersonnel weapon meant it would contribute "to the illusion that a tactical nuclear battle was fightable in the traditional sense of the term," making leaders more willing to cross the threshold between conventional and nuclear war.

Producing and deploying the neutron warhead became an issue, particularly for European governments. The calculated ambiguity concerning nuclear weapons in NATO always had required "the most careful and nuanced handling of any changes in American nuclear doctrine or deployments in Europe. Such subtlety was not possible in dealing with the ERW."[8] Schmidt came under pressure to renounce the neutron bomb. He took the position that while he could not ask for the weapon, his government would accept a deployment decision by Washington, provided one or two other NATO governments agreed.

In November 1977, Vance had recommended that the United States develop the neutron bomb and then consult Britain and West Germany to see whether they were prepared to go along. He announced the decision at a meeting of the NATO Council the next spring. The issue was debated across the Atlantic over the next months.

Vance later acknowledged that had initial interallied consultations probed deeper, they would have shown that the bomb's political liabilities outweighed its military value. Like so many decisions, it hung fire when a decision should have been taken. Vance was so busy with problems elsewhere that he did not take seriously the "continuing signs of the president's uneasiness with the program reports he was receiving."[9] The department was concerned with how to get European governments—principally West Germany—to indicate support.[10] Schmidt was under such pressure that he would not accept the political cost of deployment unless the Dutch and Belgian governments went along. American negotiators hammered on the theme that the President had decided that NATO should go forward with the neutron bomb. By mid-March 1978, after what Vance described as "a nerve-wracking week of nonstop consultations," American, British, and German officials worked out a phased plan for a preliminary meeting of the North Atlantic Council on March 20, after which it would issue a statement of support for the U.S. position.[11] The United States would proceed with the bomb while exploring the arms control aspect as a sop to European

Vance, his mother, and
brother John.

Member of the Yale
Varsity Hockey Team.

Vance and Mrs. Vance arrive in Hawaii on an inspection tour of army installations in the Pacific and Far East.

Vance (Deputy Secretary of Defense) with President Johnson.

Harold Brown, Vance, Robert McNamara, General Earle G. Wheeler
(Chair, JCS), and Arthur Sylvester. April 1966.

Vance with Carter
and Secretary of
Defense Harold
Brown at NSC
meeting.

Vance with President Carter.

Aboard Air
Force One.

Secretary of State Cyrus Vance conferring with National Security Adviser
Dr. Zbigniew Brzezinski in July 1977. "Our personal relations were
always good." From *Power and Principle: Memoirs of the National
Security Adviser 1977–1980*, published by Farrar, Straus and Giroux,
1983.

Camp David Summit—Dayan, Begin, Carter, and Vance.

Deng Xiao-ping's visit to the United States, January 1979.    Brzezinski,
Ji Chaozhu (interpreter),  Deng Xiao-ping,  and  Vance.

Weekly Friday morning breakfast session, Mondale, Vance, Carter, and Brzezinski.

Summit Meeting at Camp David—President Carter with President Sadat and Secretary of State Vance.

Meeting with Gromyko. Carter, Gromyko, Vance, and Dobrynin.

opinion. It was not required that NATO governments declare that they would accept the bomb if arms control failed; it was understood.

The preliminary meeting of the North Atlantic Council scheduled for Monday, March 20, 1978 was to precede a public announcement of a plan to produce and deploy the ERW. Over the weekend the NSC staff had briefed Carter at his retreat on St. Simon Island. Up to this point he had appeared to understand that it was his policy, and that Schmidt had gone along on the premise that the Council would ratify Carter's decision. But the President had signed off on all memos and documents not realizing that these were steps in a process leading to commitment.

Now that the decision was at hand, all of the President's reservations about ERW, moral and political, came to the fore. Perhaps he resented Schmidt's placing him in such a position. On Sunday, March 19, he ordered the scheduled NATO meeting for Monday cancelled, and the following day rejected the unanimous advice of Vance, Brzezinski, and Secretary of Defense Brown. As Vance later wrote, Carter felt that

> the burden and political liability for this weapon, which as far as he could see no ally really wanted, was being placed on his shoulders. . . .
> He appeared not to appreciate the enormous damage to his prestige and U.S. leadership that would result from backing away from the alliance consensus that had been worked out in his name.[12]

And yet he would not budge. Neither would Schmidt, who was unyielding that "Germany could not be alone in accepting deployment of the ERW on its soil."[13] Here was an example of the kind of quixotic behavior on Carter's part that frequently perplexed Vance—the onset of moral scruples, the sudden 180-degree reversal, with no regard for political costs.

Interestingly, a very similar situation had developed over the President's determination to withdraw U.S. forces from South Korea. Carter had gotten himself out on a limb on this issue. Senatorial and public clamor against an unwise or at least ill-considered move only made him dig in. Only Brzezinski supported him, and yet no one dared propose that he abandon his decision. In this regard Vance reported later that Senator Charles Percy, "a strong supporter of every other aspect of our East Asian policies," at one point had banged his fist on the table and warned of Republican opposition to a Korean withdrawal.[14] Democrats in the Senate— John Glenn, Sam Nunn, Jackson, Daniel K. Inouye, eventually Gary Hart—had joined the opposition. But as in the case of the neutron bomb, Carter had involved his sense of moral righteousness. His conviction was so intense that he could not discuss it. Only when he arrived in Seoul for a state visit and listened to General Park's harangue against withdrawal did he come to his senses. But not without Vance and others (Brown, Brzezinski, Ambassador William Gleysteen) sharing Carter's humiliation. When it became apparent that the President was ready to capitulate, Vance and Gleysteen rushed around Seoul in the embassy limousine to plead with the obdurate Koreans that Park must not press the President on the issue.[15] The state dinner that evening was a success, and three weeks later the President agreed to suspend troop withdrawals in light of intelligence, it seemed, on North Korean troop strength.

The neutron bomb and Korean fiascos showed the way the President might act toward emplacing nuclear warheads and cruise missiles in Europe. To the European demand that the U.S. do something to match the Soviet SS-20s was now added the urgent need to restore confidence in Carter's leadership. "In Washington officials resolved to reaffirm American leadership in the strongest possible way."[16] The Defense Department had been in favor of modernization ever since the High Level Group had made its recommendations. Vance and the State Department were pushed in that direction by the need to reaffirm American leadership. If European support for SALT II could be had only by reassuring the allies that their interests were not being sacrificed, then so be it. In June 1978, Carter agreed to Presidential Review Memorandum 38, entitled "Long Range Theater Nuclear Capabilities and Arms Control." Vance envisaged a policy of arming and negotiating, and yet more emphasis now came on the need to demonstrate resolve to the European allies.

Of necessity, political issues intruded on NATO military decisions. Just as modernizing NATO's nuclear weapons was not entirely justified by strategic considerations, but more out of need to meet the psychological concerns of the European allies, so the decision about the type and number of weapons to deploy was not entirely rational. Not content to go for a low number, planners had pushed for 108 Pershing IIs (each with two warheads) and 464 cruise missiles. Brzezinski summed up this problem, saying, "The question of an objective 'need' for a credible response in Europe . . . had to be balanced against internal NATO politics, various numbers dictated by a variety of actors and the need for numbers high enough to give the U.S. bargaining leverage with the Soviets."[17] But this did not even reveal the full extent to which numbers and configuration reflected interservice as well as foreign policy considerations, especially the decision to include 108 Pershing IIs so as to give the U.S. Army a piece of the NATO nuclear action.

Despite the irrational forces with which every Secretary of State must deal, Vance had still given the U.S. three years of leeway. Under the protocol to SALT II, at the end of three years the United States would be ready to deploy but also to negotiate. As is often the case, U.S. planners now became advocates of deployment of theater nuclear weapons, selling them to ever-more reluctant Europeans, brushing aside all evidence of reservations and uncertainty.

While European governments were concerned that Washington might abandon Europe's security, they were also under public pressure to avoid heightening the danger of nuclear annihilation. The West German government was bound to be sensitive to any weapon on German soil that had a first-strike capability against the Soviet homeland. Having precipitated the demand for deployment of long-range theater nuclear weapons, Schmidt was on the spot. With the Dutch and Belgian governments holding off their decision to deploy, he was under attack from the left wing of his party. A militarily superfluous weapon seemed about to wreck everything.

The attempted decision to deploy Pershing IIs and cruise missiles was an effort to meet a political and psychological problem with military hardware. It gave insufficient attention to the way in which the hardware would affect European concern with security versus détente. The Soviets now determined to exploit European misgivings. In a speech in East Berlin on October 6, 1979, with a NATO meeting two months away, Brezhnev proposed that Russia would reduce its medium-range nuclear weapons in the western part of the Soviet Union if no additional weapons were deployed in NATO countries.

As Vance had anticipated, much now depended upon the ability of the U.S. to convince its European partners, always fearful of war and anxious to preserve détente, of the American commitment to arms control. In testimony in the summer of 1979 in support of SALT II, he had warned the Senate that SALT was a part of the structure of expectations that Europeans held about United States leadership. Unfortunately the Senate's inability to see policy as a web, an interconnected political and psychological whole, was about to defeat SALT II. Without ratification it would be difficult to win European support for deployment of the new weapons.

The December 1979 meeting of the North Atlantic Treaty foreign and defense ministers adopted the American deployment plan, but with emphasis on arms control. The communiqué noted a trend toward Soviet superiority in theater nuclear systems, "highlighting the gap in the spectrum of NATO's available nuclear response to aggression."[18] It also highlighted the importance of arms control "in contributing to a more stable military relationship between East and West and in advancing the process of détente." NATO ministers regarded arms control as "part of the alliance's effort to assure the undiminished security of the member states . . . In this regard they welcome the contribution which the SALT II Treaty makes toward achieving these objectives . . ."[19] As Vance had indicated, success for America's NATO policy presumed SALT II, and negotiation of a SALT III agreement to include theater nuclear weapons.

The Soviet invasion of Afghanistan at the end of December of that year put an end to hopes for SALT II.

## CHAPTER TEN

# Rhodesia and Namibia

By his final year as Secretary of State, Kissinger had seen his policies in Africa falter and threaten to fail. National Security Memorandum 39 had determined that the United States would continue covertly to support the white colonial regimes of southern Africa, including Portuguese Angola and Mozambique, and the white states of Rhodesia and South Africa. When Portuguese rule foundered, however, the Ford administration threw support to non-Marxist factions. In January 1976, Congress, fearing a repetition of Vietnam, rejected Kissinger's proposal to increase assistance to those factions. In Rhodesia the illegal government of Ian Smith meanwhile faced a challenge from black liberation movements operating from Zambia and Mozambique. With policy in a shambles, and confronted by the possibility of expansion of Soviet and Cuban influence, Kissinger made a dramatic bid to regain initiative, and in April, 1976 in Lusaka announced support for majority rule in Rhodesia and began working for a conference to arrange a peaceful transfer of power to the black majority. Appearing to accept majority rule, Smith hoped to delay, preserving white rule and winning Anglo-American support. This was where matters stood when Vance took office.

By contrast with Kissinger, Vance believed that nationalism would override ideology and foreign influence in determining change, however radical, and in his first speech as Secretary of State he embraced the idea that American interests everywhere need not suffer as a result of radical movements. "We do not insist," he declared, "that there is only one road to economic progress or one way of expressing the political will of a people. In so diverse a continent as Africa, we must be prepared to work with peoples and governments of distinctive and differing belief."[1] Unlike Kissinger, he felt that unless the United States stood against apartheid it would not convince black African states of its commitment to racial justice. Instead of procrastinating on the Rhodesian issue, going easy on the Smith regime to win South African support, he believed that even South Africa had a stake in a settlement that would avoid a race war and eliminate Soviet and Cuban backing for the Rhodesian guerrillas.[2] In concert with British Foreign Secretary David Owen, Vance agreed to work out the transition of Rhodesia to a constitutional regime based on black majority rule. The Smith regime stepped up its effort to produce an "internal" solution by co-opting the more moderate Rhodesian black leaders like Bishop Muzorewa, while the revolutionary Patriotic Front looked to military victory. That the Patriotic Front was divided by tribal and personal differences— ZAPU, headed by Joshua Nkomo and operating out of Zambia, and ZANU headed by Robert Mugabe—prompted the Smith regime to believe that by co-opting the moderate black leadership it could win external recognition and neutralize the black nationalists.

To press the white government of Rhodesia to negotiate with black nationalists and gain African cooperation, Vance had to persuade Congress to repeal the Byrd Amendment, under which Rhodesia continued to export chrome to the United States despite U.N. sanctions. Pleading the administration's case, he made clear that while the outcome in Rhodesia had to be a fair election open to all, the United States would not agree to a transition that left no hope or safeguards for the white minority against arbitrary rule or expropriation of property. Apart from Carter's sensibility to fairness, Vance knew that Congress would not sit still for a sell-out of the white minority in Rhodesia. As in other instances, his standing with Congress served him well. The amendment was repealed.

Vance knew that each side in Rhodesia would have to realize it could not improve its position by military force. The Smith regime would have to realize that no self-serving internal settlement would end the Patriotic Front's operating from Zambia and Mozambique; and the Patriotic Front would have to realize that it could not hold support of the nearby states in a long-drawn-out war to defeat the white regime. Recognition of black rights would take time. The United States would have to communicate to the people rather than to a particular leader or party.[3] Vance also would need to convince the parties that the United States was "willing and able to use the leverage it had to punish intransigence and reward cooperation on a neutral basis."[4] To strengthen America's hand, he and U.N. Ambassador Andrew Young did what Kissinger had failed to do. They coordinated their African diplomacy with the nearby states—Zambia, Tanzania, Mozambique, Angola, Botswana, and Nigeria.[5] By Africanizing policy, he was able to bring the influence of Nigeria and the other states to bear on the Patriotic Front. At summit meetings of these states the United States would be represented, while neither the Soviet Union nor Cuba participated. He thus won their support for an Anglo-American initiative to achieve a negotiated settlement of the Rhodesian conflict.

The policy of working through influential regional nations like Nigeria—known as Presidential Decision 18—was, ironically, prepared by Brzezinski, who had proved skeptical of, if not antagonistic toward, Vance's diplomatic approach.[6] Although he did not interfere or oppose Rhodesian policy, he had expressed impatience with its slowness and doubt about its success. In his diary he wrote,

> I am beginning to lean to the notion that we ought to let the so-called internal solution surface, and let the moderate Africans take over from . . . Smith, because it is only to them that Smith can yield, and then let the internal solution . . . collapse as the more assertive Africans storm in from the outside. If we maintain a policy of benevolent neutrality we can accelerate the process . . .[7]

This was a curious assessment because benevolent neutrality was precisely what the nearby states, beset by guerrillas, could not accept. With Soviet and Cuban allies, the "more assertive" Africans would have stormed into Rhodesia, just what Vance's diplomacy was to circumvent.

What concerned Brzezinski, Anglo-American proposals for a phased transition to majority rule, became public on September 1, 1977. Disagreement centered on control over police and security forces. Smith demanded that they remain under his government;

the Patriotic Front demanded that they not. Smith took cognizance of Anglo-American proposals to find an internal solution that would preserve white power. To win Bishop Muzorewa and other black moderates he had accepted majority rule, but with the white minority retaining 28 seats in parliament—enough to provide a veto. With moderate black leadership amenable, Smith hoped to win support of parliamentary moderates and bring about the lifting of U.N. sanctions.

Smith's reforms would not end the war, but Vance acknowledged that the Smith-Muzorewa agreement was a step toward majority rule. He sensed that white Rhodesians would be more flexible if they knew they were not to be at the mercy of black liberation forces during the transition. They would have to have security. He concentrated on support for this point. In mid-April 1978, he and Foreign Secretary Owen flew to Dar es Salaam, the capital of Tanzania, where they found Patriotic Front leaders unwilling to yield to white demands that police and security forces not be under black control. Vance and Owen then flew to Salisbury, where they were greeted coolly. In the subsequent race between the Smith regime to win internal support, and the Patriotic Front to step up the guerrilla campaign, Vance continued his pursuit of a settlement. It had to come before the West lost influence with nearby states and before Congress, hostile to guerrilla terrorist tactics, rejected the administration's policy. Senator Jesse Helms of North Carolina came within six votes of gaining Senate approval of a measure that would have forced the Carter administration to lift economic sanctions against Rhodesia. The administration accepted an amendment (Case-Javits) to the International Security Act of 1978, adopted by the Senate, which empowered the President to lift sanctions after December 31, 1978, should it be determined that white Rhodesia had negotiated in good faith at an all-parties conference and then given way to a government chosen by free elections participated in by all parties and groups.

The problem was how to get the guerrillas to lay down arms and accept half a loaf when convinced that with time they could get all. Even if the two conditions of the Case-Javits amendment had been met, the war would have continued. By the autumn of 1978, large areas of western and southern Rhodesia were under martial law, with notably little effect upon the guerrillas. More Rhodesian whites were leaving. Despite economic support from South Africa and encouragement from conservative friends in the United States, the Smith regime was failing.

At this point came the Rhodesian elections, which were not quite conclusive enough to give Vance the leverage he needed. Without participation of the Patriotic Front the elections of April 1979, to fill 72 black seats in the new parliament, gave an overwhelming victory for Muzorewa's party, which captured 51 seats and two-thirds of the votes. Smith's Rhodesian Front Party won all 28 of the white seats. The results were sufficiently convincing to attract external support and bring nearer the moment when the Carter administration would have either to determine that the Case-Javits terms had been met or face intense congressional opposition. No less than five resolutions had been introduced calling for an end to sanctions. On May 15 the Senate voted, 75 to 19, to call on the President to lift sanctions.[8] Vance advised Carter not to do so, and Carter announced on June 7 that he would continue them because the new government had failed to win recognition of any other governments. The issue had become ideological, with right-wing senators rallying to support the Smith regime on the ground that it represented a moderate, democratic alternative to radical Marxists and terrorists. Carter's statement that the new regime did not meet the conditions of the Case-Javits amendment and that he had determined to do "what is right, what is decent, and what is fair" drew a hostile response. His words lent themselves to the charge that he was a prisoner of black extremists.

In congressional testimony Vance bowed to those who felt the administration biased against the Smith regime, conceding that the new arrangement represented progress. He agreed to keep sanctions under review. He succeeded in emphasizing the point that lifting sanctions would not end the war, but would only end America's effectiveness as a mediator: "Our primary national interest . . . is in a peaceful settlement. Continuing conflict would radicalize the situation further. It would deepen divisions within the country and within the regime. And it would create greater opportunities for outside intervention." To lift sanctions would undermine America's relations with Africa and undermine the initiative being undertaken by Lord Carrington, Owen's successor as foreign secretary.[9]

The Conservative victory in the British elections changed African equations, especially those of Rhodesia. Margaret Thatcher's emergence as prime minister did not yield support for Smith's internal solution. Instead of recognizing the Smith-Muzorewa government, the new foreign secretary embarked upon an initiative to end the conflict. Vance found that the Conservative government, impelled by Britain's economic stake in Nigeria and elsewhere in Africa, had no intention of excluding the Patriotic Front, knowing as Vance had argued all along that that would not resolve the conflict. London determined to make the run on its own. Rhodesia was still a British colony, and responsibility was theirs. The new Conservative leaders hoped they could put pressure on both sides to reach a compromise, although American support "was absolutely vital."[10] The neighboring states now wanted the conflict ended and were prepared to press the Patriotic Front. After months of negotiation, in the course of which both sides realized that neither had advantage, Carrington in October 1979 succeeded in obtaining support for constitutional changes to come into effect following a transition in which a British governor-in-residence would hold power. On March 4, 1980, another election gave Robert Mugabe's party 57 of 80 black seats in a new 100-seat parliament.

The outcome could not have been achieved had Carter and Vance not kept to their objectives. The settlement ended the danger of a race war and the erosion of U.S. influence. The government of Mugabe went out of its way to reassure whites that there was a place for them in Zimbabwe and that there would be no transformation of society in a Marxist direction. Vance demonstrated again that even bitter conflicts can be negotiated.

Meanwhile efforts had failed to get South Africa, which was combatting the Namibian independence movement, the South West Africa People's Organization (SWAPO) under Sam Nujoma, to agree to Namibian independence. Namibia was the former German colony of Southwest Africa, over which Pretoria held control. In support of the human rights policy with which the Carter administration hoped to win support in Africa, Vice President Mondale had met with South African Prime Minister Balthazar Vorster in Vienna.

Mondale expressed "fundamental and profound disagreement" with apartheid in South Africa: "We are of the opinion, strongly held, that full political participation by all citizens of South Africa—is essential." The United States wanted good relations with the South African white government but was not prepared to be quiet about apartheid or about Namibia or to support the Smith regime. Vorster characterized Mondale's statement as interference in the internal affairs of South Africa, and the meeting broke up. As Vance anticipated, however, Vorster's comments on Rhodesia and Namibia were restrained. Sensing that Smith's was a futile cause, and not wishing to see southern Africa engulfed in a race war, which might allow Communist penetration, Vorster informed Mondale that South Africa would

> support Anglo-American efforts to get the directly interested parties to agree to an independence constitution and the necessary transitional arrangements, including the holding of elections in which all can take part equally so that Zimbabwe [Rhodesia] can achieve independence in 1978, and peace.[11]

Vance believed that South African withdrawal from Namibia was essential if the United States was to win African support. It was his view that under pressure South Africa could see the wisdom of self-determination for Namibia. With the independence of Angola, SWAPO had set up just across the border from Namibia. Despite Pretoria's support for the anti-Marxist Angolan insurgency led by Jonas Savimbi, a guerrilla movement backed by Cubans on its Namibian border was not welcome. Pretoria embarked on an effort in Namibia analogous to what Smith was attempting in Rhodesia. Unable to win SWAPO to a transition regime for Namibia, Pretoria set out to concoct its own. At a meeting in the Namibian capital of Windhoek, at the so-called Turnhalle Conference, South Africa promoted a coalition of representatives of the white population and co-optable Namibian ethnic and tribal groups.

The Namibian situation had a bearing on various dilemmas confronting the United States in southern Africa. Vance's inclination had been to recognize the Angolan government of President Agostinho Neto. The unwillingness of the Ford administration had never made sense in terms of U.S. interest in getting Cubans out of

Angola. Neto had gone on record as supporting a settlement in Namibia. Recognition of Angola, as of Cuba, Vietnam, and the People's Republic of China, had been part of the Carter agenda and had led to a liaison mission in Cuba. But the intrusion of Soviet and Cuban forces in Ethiopia had put Carter on the defensive. He did not want to appear soft in dealing with the Soviet-Cuban presence in Angola, the strategic importance of which continued to be exaggerated out of all proportion.

What a confusion of choices! The administration had to have a strategy for Namibia, especially as it was bound to confront African demands for sanctions against South Africa, should the latter fail to grant independence to Namibia. To veto a U.N. resolution calling for sanctions would be at odds with the administration's African policy (self-determination); to support it would destroy the possibility of negotiation with South Africa and harm Western economic interests. It was not an issue on which to count on support from European and Western Hemisphere allies.

Vance was reluctant to favor economic sanctions toward South Africa that would result in a deadlock, and thus end all chance to negotiate Namibian independence.[12] He believed that even if a solution was not evident or even likely, the only way to avoid trouble was to negotiate. Negotiation continued on the Namibian front, easing pressure for drastic measures from within the African community and enabling Vance and the British to concentrate on Rhodesia, where matters began to evolve in a favorable direction.

At Vance's initiative a contact group—the U.S., Canada, Britain, France, and West Germany—invited South Africa and SWAPO to send representatives for "proximity talks" in New York. There was gradual agreement on a U.N.-supervised election for a constituent assembly that would include SWAPO. Disagreement arose over the use of U.N. forces to police the election and over the positioning of South African and SWAPO forces.[13] Vance and other leaders in the contact group flew to South Africa, where Vorster accepted the proposal for a U.N.-supervised election, provided the status of Walvis Bay, a port to which South Africa laid claim, would be negotiated after independence. On April 25, 1978, South Africa announced acceptance of a supervised election for a constituent assembly. Vance and the deputy chief of the U.S. mission to the

United Nations, Donald McHenry, met with the head of SWAPO and the Nigerian foreign minister. But then negotiations stalled, and South Africa launched a preemptive strike against SWAPO bases deep in Angola, leading to a break-off of talks and upsetting the Angolans.

At a meeting of the Western foreign ministers in Paris, Vance persuaded the group to renew pressure on South Africa. An envoy was dispatched to Luanda to persuade SWAPO representatives to support the Tanzanian proposal of a Security Council resolution for post-independence negotiation on Walvis Bay. On July 27 the Security Council endorsed the contact group's plan, including the resolution. On August 6 the U.N. special representative and staff arrived in Windhoek. South Africa rejected their assessment of requirements for a U.N.-supervised election: 400 police and 7,500 U.N. troops. Nevertheless the Security Council voted to authorize Secretary General Kurt Waldheim to arrange for the U.N. presence, and black Africans made clear that they expected the five Western powers to support sanctions if South Africa's compliance was not forthcoming.

Carter authorized Vance to seek a private meeting with Vorster in mid-October and warn that if South Africa refused a U.N.-supervised election, the United States would support economic sanctions. At a meeting of the five Western foreign ministers with the new South African prime minister, Pieter Botha (not to be confused with Roelof [Pik] Botha, who remained as foreign minister), Vance asked the new government to support a U.N.-supervised election. Again he and the other ministers acknowledged that SWAPO was not the only political party and all parties would be protected. Botha refused.

In the General Assembly the African and nonaligned states presented a harsh U.N. resolution, which the Americans managed to tone down. The U.S. and its Western allies abstained. Carter withheld Export-Import Bank financing for South Africa and warned Botha that he would support other sanctions. The Botha government yielded in principle, but talks with the South African foreign minister failed to resolve issues. Negotiations had stalemated.

Vance's patience in these seemingly hopeless efforts, to which he gave so much time, was remarkable. In southern Africa, as in the Middle East, Central America, and other parts of the world, conflicts existed that if not dealt with were likely to pose obvious threats. The U.S. could temporize, hoping the conflicts would go away. American interest in seeing Cubans out of Angola depended upon normalizing South Africa's relations with its neighbor Angola, and that depended upon Namibian independence. Left to its devices, South Africa preferred control of Namibia, but that entailed a price in lives and resources. Vance presumed that if South Africa could be persuaded that Namibian independence would enhance the security of everyone—whites and non-SWAPO blacks—he could tilt the balance in favor of settlement. He believed that the way to keep things from getting worse was to go all-out to make them better.

CHAPTER ELEVEN

# Camp David

The negotiation for an Israeli-Egyptian peace treaty in the rural atmosphere of the President's retreat at Camp David, high in the Catoctin Mountains in Maryland, near Washington, was an act of high political courage on the part of all three leaders. Each took a risk, but especially Carter. In the ten months since meeting in Jerusalem, Sadat and Begin had retreated to mutually hostile positions. Each was under domestic pressure. Vance was convinced that the time had come for the United States to end its role as mediator and advocate a position each side would have to accept if the negotiation was to succeed. There also was the possibility of an agreement involving the other Arab states. Kissinger's shuttle diplomacy had demonstrated that there was no possibility of progress without American leadership.[1] By convening the Camp David summit meeting, Carter intended to enter the negotiation.

If credit for both inspiration and courage belongs to Carter, the fact that the Camp David Conference could be held at all was due to Vance's "stick-to-it-iveness."[2] We have seen the patience (and Begin would say relentlessness) with which the secretary and colleagues chipped away at Israeli resistance. Between December 1977 and August 1978 he struggled through three negotiations—two in the Middle East and one at Leeds Castle in England. Days of preparation were spent before and after each negotiation.

Preparation for the Camp David meeting, scheduled to open September 5, 1978, was made by Vance and his associates—Hal Saunders, Roy Atherton, and William Quandt—at the Harriman's guest house in Middleburg, Virginia, where drafts of proposals were worked out. There were to be two U.S. groups at Camp David: a political team that would negotiate, consisting of Carter, Vance, Brzezinski, and on occasion Mondale and Harold Brown. The advisory team consisted of Saunders, Atherton, Quandt, and Ambassadors Samuel Lewis and Hermann Eilts. The latter would carry on parallel consultation with Israeli and Egyptian experts. The Israeli delegation was to consist of Begin, Dayan, Defense Minister Ezer Weizman, and Aharon Barak, who was the young Israeli attorney general and frequently would provide imaginative ways to overcome Begin's legal quibbles. The Egyptian delegation was to consist of Sadat, Foreign Minister Kamel (who would subsequently resign in protest against Sadat's concession), Boutros Ghali, and Osama el-Bas.

The administration had planned for a three-day conference to be extended by another four days if necessary. No one anticipated that they would be there through thirteen intense and discouraging days with success in prospect only during the final hours. Begin and Sadat arrived determined to drive a hard bargain. The first days at Camp David went in seeking to overcome the distrust between them. Begin was in the stronger bargaining position because he knew that if talks failed because of his unyielding positions on the Sinai and West Bank settlements or on his rejection of the principle that Resolution 242 meant withdrawal from all occupied Arab lands he could count on the hard-liners in Likud closing ranks behind him. Sadat had the benefit of the good will which he had won with Carter by virtue of his charm and seeming reasonableness. But it quickly became evident that the two leaders were so mutually antagonistic toward each other and so outraged by the other's intransigence, that face-to-face negotiations proved disastrous and threatened to break up the conference. Carter writes of one session, "All restraint was now gone. Their faces were flushed and the niceties of diplomatic language and protocol were stripped away. They had almost forgotten that I was there."[3]

If the conference was to be salvaged the two leaders would have to be kept apart. There then emerged one of the most remarkable arrangements in the annals of diplomacy. Carter established a working party comprised of himself, Vance, the Israeli Attorney

General, Aharon Barak, and the Egyptian Under-Secretary of State for Foreign Affairs, Osama el-Bas. "It was unheard of for a head of state to negotiate over detail in this way with two technical experts, who then had to go back and sell the agreed clause to their masters. But it worked."[4] In the course of these negotiations the other lawyer besides Vance, Barak, the Israeli Attorney General, emerged as the indispensable surrogate for Begin.

Carter, Vance, and associates shuttled between cabins of the two leaders rather than risk having them come together and fall into the vituperative exchanges that had become all too common since their initial euphoric meeting in Jerusalem. Vance and his experts produced an American text to bridge the two positions, and reviewed the rejections. This approach had the psychological advantage of making each position a rejection of the American text.[5] Questions at issue, of course, were the old ones—Israeli withdrawal from the occupied territories, a freeze on settlements on the West Bank, evacuation of all of the Sinai, the situation of East Jerusalem, and the status of Palestinians on the West Bank and in Gaza.

Carter's initial shock was to discover how far apart the sides were. In two days of marathon sessions, he and Vance worked to overcome differences. When the situation seemed hopeless, Vance reassured him that it was like most negotiations, with alternation of euphoria, depression, and despair, but with each side moving a little closer. Many of their formulas were designed to bring the sides together but also to plaster over what could not be agreed. "The central impasse was overcome by separating the Sinai issues, on which agreement seemed possible, from the West Bank and Gaza issues on which agreement on only the general principles appeared possible."[6]

Begin determined not to yield autonomy for the Palestinians, the West Bank, and Jerusalem. Tension between Americans and Israelis was extreme. On the first day Dayan tried to talk Vance into concessions on the Sinai settlements and the inadmissibility of acquisition of territory by war, a principle the Israelis wanted to disregard in contravention of U.N. Resolution 242. They wanted to retain settlements in the Sinai around El Arish. Vance "immediately and rather categorically stated that these were unacceptable."

The Palestinian issue was uppermost. No Arab government, not even Sadat's, could sign without provision for self-determination. If the Egyptian leader did not secure recognition for Palestinian rights on the West Bank, other Arab governments would say he had sold out the Palestinians. Tension was so great within the Egyptian delegation that at one point Carter feared Sadat's colleagues might kill him.[7] Foreign Minister Kamel resigned on the final day of the conference, saying Sadat had given away too much. To an ashen-faced Vance, Sadat revealed his intention of going home forthwith. Carter persuaded him to stay.

Like a lawyer, Vance stuck to his brief, rarely raising his voice but boring in. One of the first things Carter had asked Vance, following his meeting with Begin in the summer of 1977, was whether he thought Begin sincere. Brzezinski reports that Vance thought so,

> but only in his own sense in that he wishes to promote fully the rather one-sided concept of a settlement he entertains. . . . I was again struck in the course of the . . . conversation how hard-nosed Cy was in regard to the need to press the Israelis . . . in advocating self-determination for the Palestinians, including the possibility of a separate and independent Palestinian state on the West Bank.[8]

Without Vance's unrelenting pursuit of Israeli concessions, it is unlikely that Camp David would have been a success. Vance took the role of "point man," unswerving in his determination to force Begin to accept a framework for a comprehensive settlement, including autonomy for the Palestinians, not just a treaty with Egypt. If Israel wanted peace and had no intention of annexing the West Bank, why could there not be autonomy? Assuming that Begin never intended to give up the West Bank, only negotiate a peace treaty, the Israeli leader now had to confront the administration demand for some recognition of the right of Palestinians on the West Bank to self-determination and an end to Israeli settlements there or see the negotiation fail. Never had an American president and his Secretary of State so confronted an Israeli leader. Having come face to face with the President, and not wanting to lose the possibility of peace with Egypt, Begin dared not risk the negotiation. Had it been between two adversaries the intensity of feeling might not have been as great. Each would have had to agree to disagree or go to war. But this was a conflict between two virtual allies. Begin thereupon agreed to dismantle Israeli settlements in the Sinai if the Knesset approved, provided agreement was reached on other Sinai issues such as access to Sinai oil that would revert to Egypt. He also gave ground on Palestinian autonomy. Both issues were parts of a Framework for Peace in the Middle East, the American proposal.

The core of the accord, which measures how far Vance and Carter succeeded in getting Begin to accept the principle of West Bank autonomy, follows:

> Egypt and Israel agree that in order to ensure a peaceful and orderly transfer of authority . . . there should be transitional arrangements for the West Bank and Gaza for a period not exceeding five years. [This belied any Israeli intent of annexing the territory.] In order to provide full autonomy to the inhabitants, under the arrangement the Israeli military government . . . will be withdrawn as soon as a self-governing authority has been freely elected by the inhabitants of these areas to replace the existing military government.
>
> [The parties including Jordan and the Palestinians] . . . will negotiate an agreement which will define the powers and responsibilities of the self-governing authority to be exercised in the West Bank and Gaza. When the self-governing authority (administrative council) in the West Bank and Gaza is established and inaugurated, the transitional period of five years will begin. As soon as possible but not later than the third year after the beginning of the transitional period, negotiations will take place to determine the final status of the West Bank and Gaza and its relationship with its neighbors . . . the negotiations shall be based on all the provisions and principles of the UN Security Council Resolution 242. The negotiations will resolve, among other matters, the location of the boundaries and the nature of the security arrangements. The solution from the negotiations must also recognize the legitimate rights of the Palestinian people and their just requirements.
>
> . . . all necessary measures will be taken and provisions made to ensure the security of Israel and its neighbors during the transitional period and beyond . . .[9]

The world had every right to view this accord as an agreement by Israel to recognize the right of Palestinians on the West Bank and in Gaza to a transition that would eventuate in autonomy for the West Bank under terms worked out with Israel, Jordan, and representatives of the Palestinians on the West Bank. As Vance later wrote,

The Camp David accords reflected in our judgment the outer margins of the possible at the time. A review of the accords shows that Israel did recognize that the Palestinian people had 'legitimate rights,' and would be given full autonomy. Israel did commit to a process which, if faithfully implemented, would lead to the establishment of an elected Palestinian self-governing body. [10]

In retrospect one can see that Begin never intended autonomy for the West Bank even under conditions designed to provide Israel the right to protect its security interests during the five-year transition period, at the end of which it would know whether it could accept the outcome. [11] The intention of the Begin government to annex the West Bank was not apparent at the time, although the desire of Begin and his coalition partners from the National Religious Party to do so was or should have been known. Diplomacy always involves an element of chance, never more so than in a situation such as the Middle East. Given the stakes for Israel in reaching a modus vivendi with its Arab neighbors, particularly Jordan, and the significance that Palestinian autonomy for the West Bank and Gaza would have as an alternative to the Palestinian Liberation Organization, Camp David offered Israel opportunity to extend the process of peace begun with Egypt without loss of control.

The Framework for Peace in the Middle East met the Israeli preference for step-by-step, nation-by-nation settlement by limiting negotiation of the West Bank issue to representatives of the Palestinians living there and to Jordan. Had the Begin government been sincere in its promise of autonomy to West Bank Palestinians, the way would have opened for negotiation with Jordan analogous to Israel's negotiation with Egypt. Carter and Vance had done all they could.

The achievement was to be dashed by the Israelis, who refused to allow even Palestinian administrative councils or to cease construction of West Bank settlements. Although an agreement and not a treaty, it was a commitment that Israel failed to carry out, even though the Egyptian government fulfilled its obligation, under the other Camp David accord, to negotiate peace with Israel.

The peace agreement, entitled a Framework for the Conclusion of a Peace Treaty Between Egypt and Israel, provided for withdrawal of Israeli forces from the Sinai; passage by Israeli ships through the Gulf of Suez, the Suez Canal, and the Strait of Tiran; and, after a peace treaty and withdrawal of Israeli forces, normal relations between Egypt and Israel.

Letters were exchanged expressing undertakings on such controversial points as Jerusalem. Begin wrote Carter of his intention to solicit Knesset opinion on "removal of Israeli settlers from the northern and southern Sinai." A letter from Sadat to Carter reaffirmed the need for removal. Sadat wrote Carter that Egypt would assume responsibility for the Arab role stemming from the West Bank agreement.

The only letter that did not get delivered was from Begin to Carter, that Israel would establish no new settlements pending agreement on autonomy. Vance later wrote that because of this letter the U.S. had agreed to drop its own language on a moratorium.[12]

The settlement question had been the source of bitter disagreement between the Carter people and the Israelis. Although no provision was made in the actual accord for a cessation of the construction of Israeli settlements on the West Bank, it clearly constituted the most important signal that the Israelis could have given of their intention to accept Palestinian autonomy. According to Vance who took notes during the negotiation, it was agreed that "no new Israeli settlements would be established after the signing of the Framework for Peace, and that the issue of additional settlement would be resolved by the parties during the negotiations." In an interview with Eric Silver, Vance states that the American side assumed that the hold on new settlements would extend beyond the short period during which the peace treaty with Egypt was being negotiated and that the freeze would continue along with the autonomy talks. Begin rejected the idea of a document to be signed by Sadat on a settlement freeze, so Vance proposed a side letter to be drafted and signed by Begin to Carter accepting a settlement freeze coterminous with the autonomy negotiations. The Israelis are equally emphatic that they agreed only to a settlement freeze for the duration of the negotiations on the Israeli-Egyptian peace treaty and not for the duration of the autonomy talks or for the five year transition period.[13]

Had Israel been willing to live up to the agreement for West Bank autonomy, a further stage for Middle East peace might have opened, but it did at least remove the threat of another Arab-Israeli war. Israel had secured its southern border and deprived Arab states of their principal military ally. Egypt's alignment with the U.S. also increased. Camp David brought the Palestinian question to the fore. Diplomacy is the art of the possible; it hardly seemed relevant that Camp David ignored Syria and reinforced the "rejectionist front."

Vance's first task after Camp David was to negotiate the Israeli-Egyptian peace treaty, which involved parallel negotiation on Israeli withdrawal from the Sinai and the ever-elusive arrangement for West Bank autonomy. The latter was indispensable if Sadat was to escape the Arab accusation that he had sold out Palestinian rights to get the Sinai. Over the next months Vance met with the Israeli and Egyptian foreign ministers in Washington. He went to the Middle East to consult Begin and Sadat. The biggest obstacle was, of course, Israeli resistance to tying Egyptian recognition to progress on the West Bank. The Israelis refused to agree to any West Bank commitment that would compromise their control or later justify Egypt in denouncing the treaty. Begin made the situation intolerable by shamelessly arguing that while he had agreed not to start any new settlements he had not renounced Israel's right to expand existing settlements.

Progress was complicated by increasing pressure on Begin and Sadat at home—Begin's right-wing critics, Sadat's Palestinians. Egypt pressed Israel to agree to a date for completion of the autonomy talks and for holding elections for a self-governing Palestinian body on the West Bank, simultaneous with withdrawal of Israeli forces from the Sinai and recognition. This Israel rejected, demanding that the peace treaty take precedence over Egypt's defense agreements with other Arab states. Without Vance's participation, many of the deadlocks and semantic tangles would never have been resolved. Agreements reached in Washington were frequently rejected by Cairo and Jerusalem. Begin announced plans for expansion of West Bank settlements. He denied a commitment to hold a referendum for Palestinians. Sadat's vice president, Hosni Mubarak, was dispatched to Washington. Afterward Vance commented on the negotiation: "The work was appallingly tedious, but day-by-day we inched forward."[14]

For all the advantages of peace with Egypt, many Israelis opposed giving up even the Sinai settlements. Vance had to mollify Sadat while keeping pressure on Begin. Sadat on November 29, 1978 offered Begin a "personal" proposal for completing the treaty if Begin would agree to negotiate on West Bank elections and self-government by September 1979. Begin rejected the personal proposal. At this point Carter determined that Vance would have to return to the Middle East and deal with the two leaders—this in the midst of the Iranian crisis, at a time of secret negotiation with Beijing on normalization, and when Vance was preparing to meet Gromyko in Geneva on SALT.

On this inconvenient Middle Eastern trip Vance resorted to an interpretive note to ease Sadat's linkage problem, a letter from Carter declaring that the treaty was "in the context of a comprehensive peace settlement in accordance with the provisions of the Framework for Peace in the Middle East agreed at Camp David."[15] On the West Bank and Gaza issue Vance told Sadat that the U.S. "would support language in the side letter that elections would be held 'not later than the end of 1979' for the self-governing authority—but as a good-faith target, not as a deadline—and the self-governing authority would be established within one month after the elections."[16] He sought this compromise amidst a hail of Israeli recrimination touched off in part by Carter's public praise of Sadat as "generous and responsive." Called back to Washington for the President's precipitate announcement of normalization of relations with the People's Republic of China, Vance learned on the flight home that the Israeli cabinet had issued a harsh statement accusing the U.S. of a "pro-Sadat attitude." He momentarily lost his "cool" and let traveling reporters know it was the Israeli government that had prevented the negotiation from meeting the December 17 deadline set at Camp David.

The negotiation went on and on. Early in the new year (1979), following a trip by Defense Secretary Brown—prompted by the collapse of the Shah's regime and the ensuing shock to the status quo in the Persian Gulf—the administration renewed its mediation, in talks between Vance, Dayan, and Prime Minister Mustapha Khalil at Camp David in February. In early March Begin came to Washington for meetings with Carter (March 2–4, 1979) which proved to be "among the most difficult the two leaders ever had."[17]

Carter lost all patience with Begin's nitpicking and carping about Sadat, and Vance had to confess to Begin that he had exhausted his own ingenuity in searching for formulas. Begin finally accepted a Vance compromise: the peace treaty would not prevent Egypt from honoring its defense agreement with any Arab state that was a victim of aggression, but Egypt's general defense commitments would not prevail over the peace treaty. Even on this trip Begin would not agree to anything without going back to the Israeli cabinet, although he did agree to try to convince the cabinet "to accept what had started out badly and turned out well."[18] The Israeli cabinet accepted the compromises, but it was still necessary to get Sadat's acceptance. Carter determined to risk going in person to the Middle East. Begin left Washington on March 4, and Carter and Vance arrived in Cairo on March 7. The concessions asked of Sadat could not help but be painful, because they compromised the linkage between the treaty and Palestinian autonomy. But the advantages to Egypt, and to Sadat's ambition to regain the Sinai, were real. Sadat agreed that the U.S. had done its best and the time had come to sign.

Everything at long last was up to Begin. Having negotiated with Sadat, Carter and Vance flew to Jerusalem. There they encountered a suspicion that in asking for modification, the U.S. was in collusion with Egypt. To Begin's objection that he could not sign the treaty before the Knesset approved, Vance argued that there was no telling what might be said in the heat of Knesset debate. Hour after hour, meeting after meeting, Vance and Carter and aides ironed out points.[19] Israeli ministers alternated between the Americans, secret cabinet meetings, and stormy Knesset sessions. Carter and Vance hammered on compromise, while the Knesset hammered on Begin.

On March 12 haggling was still going on over the Egyptian request that parties agree to autonomy in Gaza first and over Egypt's unwillingness to give Israel access to Sinai oil. When the Israelis reported their final proposals, Vance told them he could not return with them to Cairo because the Egyptians were sure to reject them. Vance left the meeting with Begin that afternoon anguished by the thought that the two sides had come so close.[20]

Dayan and other Israeli ministers were troubled too, and proposed meeting again with Vance, and Begin agreed that Dayan should do so. As Vance sat pondering alternatives that evening the telephone rang. It was Dayan. No doubt congenialities of mind and temperament had much to do with bonds between Vance and Dayan, who was the statesman of international stature on the Israeli side. Dayan believed that Israelis and Arabs could live in peace. He still possessed the idealism of the generation of "sabras." Like Vance he had an appreciation that one could only gain by conceding. Vance and Dayan talked for several hours and arrived at a formula, and Dayan suggested that the President invite Begin to breakfast next morning. As the two leaders prepared for breakfast, Vance and Dayan disentangled the last of the knots. Enough "give" had been achieved for the President to fly back to Cairo, Khalil objected, but Sadat was not dissuaded.

On March 25, 1979, Begin and Sadat arrived in Washington. The Israelis remained contentious to the end. Nevertheless the leaders signed the peace treaty on March 26, 1979, a monument to Vance's diplomacy as much as Carter's courage.

There were no more Sadats in the Arab world who might have put Israel's claim to the West Bank to the test of diplomacy. Americans, and perhaps saddest of all, the American Jewish community, could not find it possible to recognize that the Carter-Vance performance came from the Old Testament as well as American national interest. The Framework for Peace constituted the only practical program. Vance was right that "the autonomy process provided the indispensable political basis and negotiating structure for resolving the Palestinian issue, which was the sine qua non for attempting to persuade the other Arab parties that the Camp David process could produce solutions compatible with Arab interests and dignity."[21]

While participation of the American President and Secretary of State gave credibility to Arabs and Israelis, the resentment of American Jews reinforced right-wing criticism of the administration's other policies. When advisers persuaded Carter to reduce his personal involvement in hope of regaining support of Jewish voters, hope for further progress died. Carter proposed Robert Strauss as his Middle East negotiator, in place of Vance, who could only swallow his resentment when Carter made clear that he needed Strauss as a political shield in the forthcoming election. Strauss was later succeeded by Linowitz.

In his memoirs Vance offered a prophecy on the Middle East:

> As soon as the elections were over it would be essential to give top priority to the autonomy talks and to renew the flagging momentum. Experience has taught us that matters do not stand still in the Middle East. If momentum is allowed to flag, they begin to slide backward.[22]

The tragedy was that American foreign policy in 1979–1980 had to observe the electoral season. The President abandoned the constructive policy that was producing results, so that he would not further weaken his chances of reelection. He thereby lost again.

## CHAPTER TWELVE

# SALT II (Part Two)

Despite the faulty start and the imbroglio over the Horn of Africa, progress on SALT II during 1977 gave evidence that the Soviets were as interested as the United States in moderating the nuclear arms race. While both sides wished to upgrade missile forces, each agreed to limits (and sublimits) on MIRVed missiles that represented concessions. Moscow accepted a lowering of the Vladivostok ceiling from 2,400 to 2,250, which would require reduction in Soviet but not U.S. strategic forces, and agreed to a subceiling of 1,200 MIRVed missiles within a ceiling of 1,320 MIRVed launchers. Since the Soviet Union was not expected to deploy cruise-armed bombers like the B-52, the effective MIRV launcher limit was 1,200 for the Soviet Union but 1,320 for the United States.[1]

The Soviets agreed to a sublimit of 820 MIRVed intercontinental ballistic missiles. While not as low as Vance had sought in his May 1977 negotiation, it represented a limit on numerical and throw-weight advantages in the Soviet land-based arsenal. In ensuing negotiations the Soviet Union would agree to verification that would require single-warhead versions of the SS-17 and SS-18, to be counted against the MIRV ceiling, as well as other concessions favorable to the United States. The U.S. in turn would agree to temporary restrictions on cruise deployments and other short-term restrictions on U.S. modernization. While both sides could modernize, the terms restrained Soviet strategic capability at a time when it had built up momentum. The Kremlin succeeded in delaying deployment of American land- and sea-based cruise missiles. Vance entered the second year of negotiations "feeling increasingly comfortable with Gromyko as a negotiating partner. While acknowledging that Gromyko was 'a very tough cookie,' Vance respected the foreign minister as a fellow professional."[2]

This was promising because there was bargaining still to be done. Unlike types and numbers of missiles, about which one might disagree but were not susceptible to cheating or deception, remaining issues—principally verification and modernization—involved such problems. Not only did Senator Jackson and the anti-SALT critics have to be convinced, but Brown and the JCS—a situation that gave rise to "intramural tension" within the administration.[3] Warnke in Washington (sometimes in Geneva) was charged with overseeing this nuclear chess game—with the Pentagon and Congress observing in Washington and the NATO allies as similarly nervous bystanders. The enemies of SALT had a Trojan horse in Geneva in the form of General Edward Rowny, who at the critical moment would resign, denounce the treaty, and defect to the camp of the treaty's opponents.[4]

While Vance had in Warnke a reliable surrogate (of far too much intellectual nimbleness to suit critics), the secretary had to defend Warnke's moves against the Pentagon and take responsibility for defending the game's result in the Senate. Already a campaign was underway led by the Committee on the Present Danger, headed by Nitze and Eugene Rostow, to discredit the treaty before an American public provoked by Soviet moves in Africa and reverting to its traditional distrust of Soviet intentions.

Several factors made negotiation more difficult. Vance arrived for a meeting in Moscow almost directly from negotiation in southern Africa—from Dar es Salaam to Pretoria to Salisbury—in "a strenuous but futile effort to play midwife to the peaceful birth of Zimbabwe."[5] Another distracting issue was the European demand, especially urgent after Carter's abandonment of the neutron bomb, that the U.S. consider transferring plans and technology of cruise missiles to Europe to offset the so-called "Euro-strategic imbalance" presumed to have developed with Soviet deployment of the SS-20. The Soviets were determined to invoke Article IX of the 1972 antiballistic missile treaty forbidding the U.S. to transfer new missile systems like the cruise. "The meeting produced a hard won victory for the Americans on this issue . . ."[6] The Soviets dropped their demand for prohibition of transfer systems in favor of an American clause against circumvention of the obligations (principally strategic limits) of the treaty "through any other state or states."

But the worst of the difficulties in negotiating SALT II was the deterioration in U.S.-Soviet relations largely because of changes in American public opinion. Carter would not only have to maintain his determination not to invoke linkage but would have to convince the public that Soviet and Cuban activities in Angola and Ethiopia were not so serious as to justify breaking off SALT or polarizing Soviet-American relations. To educate the public to accept risk and challenge in relations between the superpowers without abandoning pursuit of nuclear arms control would have been a tall order for any President. American opinion was swinging away from its post-Vietnam, post-Watergate mood. The right-wing was exploiting this shift to discredit administration policies. Feeling himself on the defensive, Carter was coming under pressure from Brzezinski to toughen his talk and make progress on SALT conditional on Soviet acquiescence in détente and human rights.

This situation highlighted the differences between Vance and Brzezinski that had come into the open during the Ethiopian crisis.[7] Gone was the mutually appreciative outlook with which Carter's two top advisers had taken up their roles. The differences lay not so much in their view of the Soviet Union as a competitor determined to be equal but in their view of Soviet intentions and how best to respond, and in Brzezinski's ambition to supplant Vance.

Vance disagreed with Brzezinski over the importance of Soviet and Cuban activities in Angola and Ethiopia. He disagreed that Soviet activities were the cause of the conflict or that challenging them could eliminate conflict. What Brzezinski defined as a Soviet design or strategy for world expansion may have been seen in Moscow as a response to an American strategy for resolving Third World conflicts on terms favorable primarily to the U.S. Vance did not see in every Soviet gain a challenge to American credibility. Implicit in Vance's reluctance to apply linkage to SALT II was belief that, while the Soviets would act where opportunity arose, there was no way the U.S. could force the Kremlin to desist by threatening to abandon SALT. Vance had trouble with Brzezinski's view that the Soviet Union had unlimited expansionist ambitions and could be made to back down in situations in which the balance of costs and risks was slight. That would lead to bluffing at the expense of achieving a possible compromise. Vance could have inquired why if the Soviet Union could be warned off by linkage did Brzezinski see unlimited expansion as a Soviet motive.

If the administration meant what it said about accepting competition in Soviet-American relations, what else was Soviet activity in the Horn of Africa or Yemen or Angola if not competition? If the administration was as confident of advantage in the competition as it had every right to be in light of Soviet failure to consolidate its ties to a host of countries—China, Egypt, Guinea, Somalia—then it need not view every Soviet gain as permanent defeat.

Brzezinski persisted and, to chasten the Soviets, recommended that the U.S. make Soviet respect for human rights part of the ideological competition and enter upon new (and provocative) initiatives in such areas of Soviet sensitivity as China.[8] Such was the conflict generated by the Adviser for National Security. Given the mood in the country and in Congress, his call for a tougher policy was bound to appeal to Carter, who felt frustrated by the Kremlin's failure to confirm his view that Soviet-American relations would improve once he became President. Although Carter deferred to Vance's advice on most issues, Brzezinski was no longer merely helping the President "facilitate the process of decision," as he had proclaimed his function, but challenging the Secretary of State. Fourteen members of the House International Relations Committee sent the President a letter in June, 1978 asking him to clarify "U.S. policy on such issues as Soviet-American relations and Africa." The conflict was tailor-made for exploitation.[9] Vance's reluctance to speculate about policy put him at a disadvantage.

At the same time that Brzezinski was challenging Vance, he was not performing his own role adequately. A study commissioned by Carter as part of his Reorganization Project found Brzezinski neglecting the organizational side. The NSC staff had failed in its institutional performance because of preoccupation with advice to the President.[10]

To persuade Carter not to succumb to the hostility toward the

Soviet Union found increasingly among the public, and promoted within the White House, Vance sent the President a message that the national mood arose from impatience with the intractability of international problems, from the high level of Soviet involvement in Africa, and from public reaction to the argument that the United States had become less resolute.[11] He urged Carter to resist those advisors who proposed to increase tension. To offset weakening public support, he proposed that the administration continue to pursue SALT II in combination with a prudent increase in defense spending along lines proposed by Defense Secretary Brown. Vance argued that Brzezinski's public criticism fed the inevitable public disenchantment instead of making the best case for the President's policies. He recommended demonstrating confidence in the competition with the Soviet Union, and at the same time easing the human rights strictures that were only causing the Kremlin to crack down on dissidents.[12] Proposing that the President give an address, Vance had a speech prepared for delivery at the Naval Academy commencement, June 7. Brzezinski gave Carter another draft. Instead of deciding what theme he wanted, Carter drew from both.[13] The differences of approach that were apparent confirmed the public impression of an administration and president unable to decide on a consistent course.

Among recommendations that Vance had made to Carter was that he should manage the U.S.–China relationship so as not to give the impression of playing China off against the Soviet Union. The Soviet Union was the other superpower, not China. While normalization was important, it should not be sought at the expense of more important considerations. In a memo to Carter a year earlier, April 15, 1977, Vance had suggested that, "The principal condition for good relations with the People's Republic of China will be to convince the Chinese that the Administration has a mature and realistic view of the world situation and strategic balance."[14]

Meanwhile Brown had joined Brzezinski in arguing for a security relationship with China involving arms. Vance warned that "This approach could be quite dangerous and going very far down that road would pose real risks. Nothing would be regarded as more hostile to the Soviet Union than the development of a U.S.–Chinese security relationship."[15]

These differences might have come to contention on the eve of Vance's trip to Beijing that summer of 1977, had not both Vance and Brzezinski agreed that the administration had too many issues before Congress. Nothing came of Vance's trip because of Beijing's unwillingness to tolerate America's continued commitment to the security of Taiwan.

The China issue reappeared in March 1978, almost as a sequel to the Horn of Africa, when Brzezinski began a campaign to resurrect strategic military consultations with the Chinese to "balance the Soviets," and also to secure presidential approval for a personal trip to China.[16] The campaign provided a remarkable study in bureaucratic politics. First he spoke to the Chinese Liaison Mission in Washington, securing an invitation to China.

> I made a sustained effort to obtain Presidential approval of my trip to China. . . . I had become quite preoccupied with Moscow's misuse of détente to improve the Soviet geopolitical and strategic position around Saudi Arabia. . . . to overcome State's resistance, I had to fashion an alliance . . . first I prevailed on Mondale to talk to the President.[17]

The President acceded to Brzezinski's importunities and his visit was set for May. Vance might have considered resigning. Having justified the trip as consultative, the President, in another of his 180-degree reversals, determined it should be "a serious and substantive occasion."[18] Brzezinski was to address the question of normal relations. Carter told Brzezinski to write his own instructions, which he proceeded to do in the most expansive terms: "You should state that the United States has made up its mind and is prepared to move ahead with active negotiations to remove the various obstacles to normalization." Among the obstacles were those concerning relations with Taiwan, a subject on which Congress expected to be consulted. Instead of allowing the security treaty with Taiwan to lapse, it was to be abrogated; and instead of Congress being consulted, it was to be kept uninformed.

In Beijing, Brzezinski let himself get carried away with exhilaration at having capped Kissinger's performance. Not content with the possibility of a Sino-American alignment, he included in his formal toast at a state banquet the admonition that "Only those aspiring to dominate others have reasons to fear the further development of American-Chinese relations."[19] He used a much publicized visit to the Great Wall "to make a number of unabashedly anti-Soviet remarks," and capped it off by describing the Russians as "international marauders" for their policies in Africa. It is hard to imagine a performance that could have been more to the delight of Beijing and detriment of the U.S. What could be more to the advantage of China, which had little to offer, than to have the United States falling all over itself? What more disgraceful than to have Deng giving a representative of the President lectures on "the disadvantages of SALT to the U.S."? The Chinese must have felt in seventh heaven.

If it was possible the situation worsened when, in a *Meet the Press* interview shortly after his return, Brzezinski depicted the Soviet Union as the world's troublemaker and concluded that its behavior was incompatible with "what was one called the code of détente."[20] Next morning's *Washington Post* headline read "Brzezinski Delivers Attack on the Soviets," and said it meant he had become the adviser to Carter, overshadowing Vance, unless the President disowned him. Even Carter's ire was roused. For once he seemed to sense the implications of having a loose cannon (in this case a professor) in the White House. He should have been aware that anything his Assistant for National Security said in public would seem to come from the President. But nothing more happened, other than that Carter made clear that Brzezinski was not speaking for him. "Vance was deeply upset," Brzezinski reported in his memoirs, "and called to tell me so. He stated that the administration should speak with one voice. . . . I pointed out to Cy that I felt that I had spoken in keeping with the President's position."[21]

All the while disagreement was emerging between Vance and Brzezinski, supported this time by Brown, over the sale of military equipment and dual-use technology to China. Vance was against it, believing that the United States should deal evenhandedly with Communist powers. Brzezinski and Brown eventually convinced Carter to go ahead.

A meeting of Vance with Gromyko in July 1978 produced an important agreement on modernization of ballistic missiles, something Kissinger had been criticized for ignoring. Modernization involved such issues as throwweight, megatonnage, fractionalization (warheads), and accuracy of Soviet ICBMs. All too often, technological improvements outpaced agreements. The Vladivostok agreement had done nothing to constrain modernization. As part of the three-year interim agreement, the U.S. had proposed a ban on testing "new types" of missiles. The Soviets had held out to test a solid-fueled, single-warhead missile to replace the SS-11. It then became apparent that with cancellation of the B-1 and with Soviet heavy missiles (first strike) becoming an issue within the Pentagon and with critics of SALT II, the U.S. would have to counter with its own "heavy"—namely the MX (so named when it had been an experimental missile) with ten warheads. The administration decided to accept development of one new missile by each side. Now it was the Soviets' turn to decry the American intention to build a "first-strike knockout punch." The Kremlin proposed no new-missile testing for the entire treaty period. The Soviets would live without their solid-fuel, single warhead follow-on to the SS-11 if the U.S. gave up the MX.[22] But the administration was in no position to accept a ban on the MX, and the breakthrough in July 1978 consisted of agreement by Gromyko permitting each side to develop one new system, provided the U.S. was prepared to give in on other issues.

By September and another meeting with Gromyko in New York, relations had improved. Jewish emigration was at its highest level, and Soviet dissidents were receiving lighter sentences. The Soviets indicated that normalization with China would be acceptable so long as it did not appear anti-Soviet. Gromyko demanded that the U.S. agree to a strict, straight-line range limit of 600 kilometers on ground- and sea-launched cruise missiles. This reflected Soviet desire to limit the vulnerability of Soviet territory. Vance accepted this limit knowing it would expire at the end of three years; meantime he hoped to see intermediate-range theater nuclear weapons included in SALT III.

The most difficult part of SALT II negotiations that autumn involved verifiability and Soviet encryption of missile telemetry. An important means to know whether the Soviets were testing missiles was to monitor the missile's flight guidance through remote telemetry. The way to block this information was known as encryption.

Vance knew that SALT II opponents would raise this issue. Despite apparent agreement, which Warnke had worked out with Soviet negotiators, Gromyko at first rejected the agreement, and it required every bit of Vance's argumentation to persuade him that the treaty would only deny the Soviets the right to impede verification of weapons covered by the SALT II accords.

Vance returned from Moscow that October of 1978 hopeful that issues could be settled in time for the December meeting and that leaders of the two governments could hold a summit meeting early in 1979, but fate in the form of China normalization intervened. Members of Congress with oversight for U.S.–Asia relations had been briefed about American approaches to negotiation, although they did not know the administration intended to abrogate the security treaty with Taiwan. They knew, as did the public, from Vance's and Brzezinski's visits to China, that the governments could only be negotiating what had been incomplete in 1972. There was nothing secret about the matter, as had been the situation antecedent to Kissinger's flight to Beijing in the summer of 1971. Polls in 1977 and 1978 had shown that a majority of Americans favored full diplomatic relations with the PRC. A majority of about the same size, however, opposed a break with Taiwan. Congress expected to be consulted, and the more the terms of normalization departed from expectation with regard both to Taiwan and Sino-American relations the more severe would be the shock and the more divisive the debate. For this reason Vance argued that the Taiwan security treaty must lapse and not be abrogated (upon a year's notice), and normalization should be nothing more than that. To let normalization become part of an anti-Soviet strategy would disturb the balance necessary to America's relations with the Soviets.

In the autumn of 1978 the chairman of the subcommittee on Asian and Pacific Affairs of the House Committee on Foreign Affairs, Representative Lester Wolff, stressed that Congress and the American people "*must* have all the information they need to assess whether the initiatives and advances made by the administration in relation to China are acceptable."[23] He held that the nonbinding resolution passed by Congress as an amendment to the International Security Assistance Act of 1978 specified consultation prior to any changes affecting the defense agreement with Taiwan. Vance argued within the administration that not informing Congress would produce a backlash. Brzezinski said that information inevitably would leak, and Carter eventually agreed with him.[24] When Ambassador Leonard Woodcock in Beijing met with Deng, the latter suddenly wanted immediate announcement of normalization—no doubt with the intent of provoking trouble between the superpowers. Fearing a leak and anxious for a dramatic policy coup, Carter determined to oblige and released the announcement December 15, together with an invitation to Deng to visit the U.S.

And so Carter had done it—normalization was a fact. Brzezinski was ecstatic—it would "alter significantly the global balance of power."[25] The President, he wrote later, had "reviewed the normalization documents line-by-line, a picture of casual intensity"[26]—this was typical of Carter's blind spot, a preoccupation with minutiae at the expense of the wider picture. How, he might have asked, were the Soviets going to respond to this cozying up to the Chinese? What would be the view on the Hill when he sprang normalization on Congress?

Brzezinski's happiness was complete. The afternoon of December 15, 1978, he called Dobrynin to the White House for a chat

and then out of the blue I informed him that we [were] announcing . . . full scale relations with the People's Republic of China. He looked absolutely stunned. His face turned kind of gray and his jaw dropped. . . . I added that it wasn't directed against anyone and that American relations with China would now have as normal a character as Soviet relations with China. Formally, a correct observation; but substantively, a touch of irony.[27]

It is hard to imagine what compulsion underlay Brzezinski's glee at having such fun, at the expense of the Soviet ambassador and of American policy.

Incredibly, this occurred little more than a week before Vance was to go to Moscow to discuss SALT II. When he arrived on December 22, he found Gromyko angered by a reference in the U.S.–PRC joint communiqué to "mutual opposition to hegemony." The timing had offended grossly the Soviets and served to undercut relations just when SALT II was in its final stage. Agreement still might have been possible, had both sides not stuck on the telemetry issue. Gromyko agreed to accept the compromise on encryption. Vance cabled Washington for authority to resolve the issue on the basis of the compromise, only to have Washington qualify his authority. The director of the Central Intelligence Agency, Stansfield Turner, insisted that telemetry encryption as practiced in recent Soviet missile tests would violate the ban on concealment. Vance had to inform Gromyko that Carter would make this statement to Brezhnev at the summit. "We were also insisting," he afterward wrote, "that the Soviets conceded, even before the treaty was in force, that past encryption practices would be in violation of it. Gromyko refused to respond to my statement."[28]

Vance recognized that he needed to treat verification with care, for the Secretary of Defense, joint chiefs, and Turner would all have to testify without reservation that there was no way the Soviets could cheat. Anything less than candor would be unacceptable. Meanwhile the tone of negotiations was turning rancorous. The Soviets had challenged the U.S., claiming that environmental covers on Minuteman silos at Malmstrom Air Base interfered with national technical means of verification. The U.S. had raised similar challenges to two Soviet missile fields, about which suspicion or confusion existed. The concern over telemetry encryption, however, was of a differing order—it exemplified nearly insurmountable obstacles that weapons technology could place in the way of arms control. And instead of waiting as Vance preferred until after signature of SALT II, Carter had felt compelled to bring the encryption issue into the open.

In the course and sequels of this grand confusion, the provocative way in which Brzezinski had managed China normalization, at Russia's expense, gave the Kremlin incentive to delay. Brzezinski argued in his memoirs that the precipitate decision to recognize the People's Republic did not harden Soviet attitudes, and cited a conversation with Dobrynin. President Carter's memoirs did not agree, for on December 27, 1978, Carter received a letter from Brezhnev warning that unless the United States prevented its European allies from selling weapons to China, there might be no progress on SALT II. "It was obvious that the Soviet leaders were more concerned about our relations with China than we had supposed."[29]

Deng Xiao-ping arrived in the United States in February, 1979 and received a royal welcome. Instead of showing solicitude for his host's diplomatic relations with the Soviet Union, he seemed to go out of his way to be provocative. In public statements he questioned the SALT agreement and fulminated against Vietnam, with whom the Soviet Union had recently signed a security treaty. The American people were not to know at the time, but Deng informed Carter, Vance, and Brzezinski that China intended to "teach Hanoi a lesson" by a punitive invasion. The attack began February 17. While the administration did everything to minimize its effect on relations with both China and the Soviet Union, the latter might well have attacked China in support of its Vietnam ally. The Chinese called off the invasion after ten days, but not before Beijing had demonstrated the inadequacy of its forces. It was puerile for Brzezinski to believe that making the enemy of my enemy my ally automatically added to the geopolitical balance. Despite its 3,000-mile frontier with Russia, China added little weight to the superpower balance, and actually subtracted from it by fueling Russian insecurity.

Vance resumed the SALT II negotiation with Dobrynin that spring of 1979 and brought the two sides to agreement. On June 18 the President and Brezhnev signed the treaty in Vienna. They registered the understandings that did not appear in its text. The Soviets acknowledged that they were prohibited from evading telemetry needed to verify the treaty, and Brezhnev confirmed that the Soviet Union would limit annual production of the Backfire bomber to thirty aircraft. The sharpest exchanges occurred over activities disturbing to the U.S. in the Third World. Carter criticized Cuban forces in Africa; Brezhnev stiffly responded that the Soviet Union was not to blame for every Third World challenge. Both sides recognized that the next round would have to include theater nuclear forces—actual or threatened deployment of highly accurate intermediate-range missiles such as the Soviet SS-20 and the American Pershing II and cruise missiles.

For Vance, the Camp David accords, signing of the SALT II agreement, and progress on Rhodesian negotiation marked a culmination of two productive years. Unfortunately, the American people, frustrated by events in faraway Iran and Africa dismissed these achievements. The struggle continued between the Secretary of State and Brzezinski, the latter now backed by Brown and Vice President Mondale, over policy toward the People's Republic of China. Brzezinski challenged Vance's "evenhandedness," arguing that China was the weaker of the two large Communist states and ought to have favored treatment. Debate arose over whether China should receive most-favored-nation status in trade with the United States, at a time when the U.S. had denied such treatment to the U.S.S.R. Brzezinski urged this concession, supposedly to give Mondale something to communicate during a visit to China set for the end of August. Vance grudgingly agreed to have Mondale inform the Chinese that the administration would propose such treatment before the end of 1979, hoping that by then Congress would have approved the SALT II treaty. Also about this time Brown and Brzezinski joined forces in pushing a strategic targeting doctrine that emerged a year later as Presidential Directive 59. The alleged merit of the new directive was that it moved away from the notion of nuclear war as an apocalyptic conflict, to "flexible use of our forces, strategic and general purpose, on behalf of war aims that we would select as we engaged in conflict."[30] Here too Vance had doubt. On the face of it a reaffirmation of Schlesinger's selective counterforce doctrine, it was a long step in the direction of the "war-fighting, war-winning" strategy later adopted by the Reagan administration.[31] Carter, increasingly sensitive to charges that the administration was "soft on defense," was now persuaded that one way to strengthen SALT II would be Brzezinski's "hard line" approach.

# CHAPTER THIRTEEN

# *The Fall of Two Dictators*

When Vance first met the Shah of Iran, on May 13, 1977, he found him eager for Western and especially American approval and support, but "worried that many in the Carter administration, particularly President Carter, considered him a tyrant."[1] Everyone but the Shah recognized that he was a tyrant. Brzezinski wrote that after two meetings "the Pahlavis reminded me of Western-type *nouveaux riches,* obviously relishing the splendors of wealth and a Western life style, but at the same time the Shah clearly seemed to enjoy being a traditional Oriental despot, accustomed to instant and total obedience from his courtiers." The Shah, he said, "displayed megalomaniacal tendencies."[2] Carter wrote that the Shah believed suppression was the best response to opposition, and was "somewhat scornful of Western leaders (including me) who did not emulate his tactics."[3] His cultivation of an imperial style masked a flawed personality, weak and indecisive in the hour of crisis.

Americans, curiously, had confused the Shah's importance with that of his country. Because of its strategic location, Iran had figured importantly in postwar containment strategy. Nixon and Kissinger had proclaimed the Shah the surrogate for American power in the Persian Gulf. Here was a perfect example of the pernicious influence of geopolitical abstractions. They blinded American policy for a decade to what was going on in Iran. As part of the Nixon-Kissinger understanding, the American government pledged the Shah unquestioning support and had no contact with the opposition.[4]

The first thing Vance had observed about the Shah was that he was so deeply insecure that he depended upon unquestioning approval and deference from the United States. He could not tolerate the least criticism from American officials, even in private. The second thing Vance beheld was that while the Shah was familiar with international issues far from Iran, and had an unlimited appetite for sophisticated American weapons, he had no appetite for matters close to home that "depended on his personal decision"— namely, the increasing chaos of Iranian society. To the Shah it was neither necessary nor appropriate for the United States to worry about Iran's domestic situation. "He had no objection to our human rights policy, he said, as long as it was a question of general principle and not directed at him or did not threaten his country's security."[5]

Were it not for the rise in oil prices of 1973, the Shah might not have tried to transform Iran into the Prussia of the Middle East. Oil wealth and the American military connection created a relationship hideously destructive. It fueled a grossly uneven economic development and an unconscionably wasteful arms buildup. When oil prices took a tumble in 1977, he responded by cutting back in ways that affected the expectations of the populace. That was the same year, however, that he marked $5.7 billion for purchase of U.S. weapons.[6]

Because of the magnitude of American involvement and the Shah's sensitivity to criticism, talk of human rights or cutbacks in arms had to be managed so as not to disturb the Shah's equanimity. Gary Sick, the NSC staffer concerned with Iran, later observed that the United States had "become hostage to the Shah, to his particular view of the world, and in some respects to his concept of Iranian and U.S. interests."[7] Many Americans, including promoters of military sales, shared the Shah's outlook on domestic matters. Many others accepted his geopolitical view, which held Iran indispensable to containment. Last, there was a palpable determination, by everyone but a few outside specialists, to deny that something might be dangerously disjointed—between American theories of political and economic development, on the one hand, and on the other a certain willful ignorance of conditions inside Iran. Officials were prone to rationalize that political "irregularities" in Iran were part of modernizing—messy but unavoidable.

For a combination of reasons the Carter administration inherited a policy in the Gulf that discouraged the kind of intelligence gathering or continuing evaluation that might have alerted the government. Vance was sufficiently tuned in to the dilemmas of the relationship that he became cautious, but he did little to change anything. At the annual meeting of the Central Treaty Organization in London on April 19-20, 1978, he went out of his way to say that "Iran is playing a most valuable role in promoting regional progress and security."[8]

Meanwhile he instructed the political military bureau of the State Department to calculate how to limit the Shah's purchase of military equipment. This may not have been apparent when the administration went to Congress on July 7, 1977 with a request for sale to Iran of seven AWACs. Doubtful of Iran's political stability, Congress challenged the security of sensitive, supersecret AWAC technology. So intense was opposition to the sale that the administration had to reintroduce it later, at which time it received reluctant approval. The unappreciative Shah grumbled about having his desires challenged. Behind the scenes Vance approved a joint U.S.–Iranian consultative arrangement under which the American ambassador and military mission in Iran worked with the Iranian military to limit sales to what Iran could absorb "while avoiding the perception in the Shah's mind that we were altering or downgrading the basic security relationship."[9] This procedure had hardly begun when violent popular demonstrations began, demonstrations that would consume the Shah's regime and much of the Carter Administration's credibility both in Iran and with the American people.

Outbreaks of violence had begun in the spring of 1978 but, Vance later wrote, every agency of American intelligence—the embassy, experts in the department, the CIA—assured him and the President that the Shah was not in danger.[10] Ambassador William Sullivan returned from leave in late August 1978 to find the Iranian populace seething over an apparent act of arson in a theater in Abadan—a fire in which three hundred people burned to death. The Shah asked Sullivan if the demonstrators were not part of a CIA plot to overthrow his rule. Was Washington not about to make a deal with Moscow to partition Iran? All the bizarre traits of the Shah's personality came into view as the pressures on him increased.[11] A few days later the regime suppressed the demonstrations, killing several hundred protestors. The Carter administration should have realized the inescapable fact that the Shah was helpless: he could neither bring himself to ruthless repression nor abandon power to a moderate, secular opposition that might have appeased opinion and had some chance of neutralizing the religious opposition. The administration did nothing.

The Camp David negotiations were engaging Vance when the initial outbreak occurred. His views were such that he again found himself a protagonist in a duel with Brzezinski. He recommended support for the Shah but opposed President Carter authorizing the Shah to crush the insurrection. On November 2, 1978 Vance concurred in a message to Sullivan to tell the Shah that

> the United States supports him without reservation in the present crisis. . . . We also recognize the need for decisive action and leadership to restore order and his own authority. With respect to the coalition government alternative, our position is that this is up to the Shah if he feels such an alternative is viable and preferable. We are not pressing for it. The same applies to a military government. Whichever route he goes *we will support his decision fully*. (FYI: in response to your question: a military government under the Shah is *overwhelmingly preferable* to a military government without the Shah.)[12]

Brzezinski went much farther than the Secretary of State. He later admitted that he, the Assistant for National Security, had given the Shah ample support for a military crackdown. On November 3 he informed the Shah on the telephone that

> the United States supports you without any reservation whatsoever, completely and fully. . . . You have our complete support. . . . Secondly, we will support whatever decision you take regarding either the form or composition of the government that you decide upon. And thirdly, we are not, and I repeat, not encouraging any particular solution.[13]

The Shah remonstrated that "he had been made to feel that extreme measures if at all possible should be avoided," to which Brzezinski responded that, "It is a critical situation . . . and concessions alone are likely to produce a more explosive situation." The Shah asked him to repeat this statement.[14]

The Shah would not take action unless the Carter administration ordered him, which was what Vance cautioned the President against. He received every encouragement in Carter's public statements. It was the occasional intimation from the embassy that the Shah's days might be numbered that first aroused Carter's antipathy toward Sullivan. The administration wanted to believe that the Shah would get the situation under control.

In the wake of the November 2 cable and Brzezinski's telephone call, the Shah addressed the Iranian people, announcing that he would continue democratic reforms, but also establishing a military government with General Azhari as Prime Minister. The Shah never made clear to Azhari what he was supposed to do, and Azhari suffered a heart attack in early December and had to withdraw.

Brzezinski, believing the State Department and Ambassador Sullivan to be unenthusiastic in support of the Shah, opened secret conversations in Washington with Ambassador Ardeshir Zahedi in a farcical personal effort to stiffen the Shah. Vance, meanwhile, was concerned for the safety of the 20,000 American civilians living in Iran, but Brzezinski felt that evacuation would indicate the United States was pulling out.[15] On November 9 a Sullivan cable entitled "Thinking the Unthinkable" advanced the hypothesis that, short of decisive action, the Shah could not survive, and the United States had better consider an accommodation. Vance saw this cable as an assessment of the situation as Sullivan saw it; Brzezinski did not. In retrospect it is hard to see what Brzezinski expected of Sullivan. Brzezinski himself knew that Washington intelligence evaluations of Iran were worthless.[16] What better information could he get than from the American ambassador who was in day-to-day touch with the Shah and military? But to Brzezinski, Sullivan's cable was another example of State Department hostility toward the Shah.

At this point Brzezinski endorsed a recommendation that he came to repent, that George Ball should come in for a few weeks to "develop a long-term program and then perhaps even go to Teheran to sell such a program to the Shah." Nothing indicated better how far out of touch the American government was with events in Iran. Ball arrived at the same conclusion as Vance, that the Shah should appoint a coalition government and relinquish some power. He also tipped Vance off that Brzezinski was carrying on secret communications with the Shah through Ambassador Zahedi, the Shah's former son-in-law.

Throughout these weeks Vance adhered to the position that it would be immoral and unwise for Carter to take responsibility for asking the Shah to crush the insurrection. Vance's role admittedly was intermittent—he was negotiating the Egyptian-Israeli peace treaty, flying to the Middle East, and preparing for another round of SALT II in Moscow. Consonant with Ball's recommendation and with what was happening in Teheran (after General Azhari's stroke), the administration proposed that the Shah determine whether he should reinforce a military regime or move toward a civilian government. The message, to be relayed by Sullivan, was entitled "Questions for the Shah." This exercise again demonstrated how out of touch Washington was.

Undersecretary Christopher proposed a cable encouraging the Shah to form a coalition government. Brzezinski objected that it would destroy the loyalty of the army. There was nothing at this point to indicate that the army commanders had the will to do anything but survive.

Brzezinski on December 28 succeeded in overcoming Vance's hesitation to encourage the Shah to crush the opposition, and a cable went out that "the Shah should choose without delay a firm military government which would end disorder, violence and bloodshed."[17] Yet just as the Shah was receiving this message "he was moving in the opposite direction . . . he had ordered the leader of the National Front, Shapour Bakhtiar, to form a new government."[18] One of Bakhtiar's conditions was that the Shah leave Iran. It was now Brzezinski's turn to argue that the U.S. must not take responsibility for a decision the Shah alone should make. Meanwhile, in a last-minute attempt to stiffen the Iranian military, General Robert Huyser was ordered to fly to Teheran from NATO headquarters and establish liaison with Iranian commanders.

While the purpose of the Huyser mission that was publicly given out was to help the Iranian military preserve the Bakhtiar government once the Shah left, privately Brzezinski stressed that Huyser should prepare the Iranian military for a coup. As the Shah prepared to leave Iran, Sullivan notified Vance that the military had decided to crack down and prevent the departure. Vance reached

Carter and Brzezinski on Guadeloupe where they were attending an economic summit with British, French, and German leaders. He recommended that the Shah leave and that the military support Bakhtiar. Instead Carter instructed Vance to notify Sullivan not to interfere with the projected coup and that the State Department should prepare to back it. Brzezinski was delighted and reminded Carter that world politics is "not a kindergarten."[19]

Another conflict developed between Vance and Brzezinski on January 10, 1979, when Vance, on the recommendation of Sullivan, proposed that the United States make contact with the Ayatollah Khomeini in Paris. Hardly had the long-time foreign service officer Theodore Eliot prepared to go to Paris than Carter reversed himself and canceled the mission, another example of those stunning reversals to which he was susceptible. This decision, with which Vance reluctantly concurred, triggered a violent reaction from Sullivan, that offended the President. Sullivan had been struggling to keep Washington informed, advise the Shah, meet with the moderate opposition, and evacuate 20,000 Americans—all under seige conditions.

Brzezinski has written that revolutions are only inevitable after they happen. Accidents and personalities play a part. If Kerensky, for example, had had the courage to crush the Bolsheviks, Lenin would never have made it.[20] Unfortunately the Shah was the weak link in Brzezinski's strategy. Brzezinski also seemed to have confidence that the Iranian Army could control the insurrection. What was an army for if not to maintain the state? Unlike the situation in 1953, the generals supporting the Shah were not leading the army. By 1978 the Shah had the generals he wanted, which guaranteed they would be neither resolute nor competent. As in every other area in Iran, thirty years of misrule had undermined the army.

Vance's strategy was equally flawed. The notion of a coalition of moderate civilians was a chimera. The government would have had to release the nationalist leader Sanjabi from jail. Neither Sanjabi nor Bakhtiar nor any of the traditional nationalists possessed any organization or mass following. The Sullivan option of a coalition between the army and such representatives of Khomeini as Bazargan was also unlikely.

Brzezinski proclaims that his view of "a more decent world order" did not preclude use of force.[21] That leaves the question of what our interests in Iran were. The Shah's regime which was to be the means of assuring stability in the gulf had been undermined for over a decade, partly by our doing, partly the Shah's. As the situation deteriorated, the purpose shifted: the means—the Shah's regime— became the end. This was the logical conclusion of the pernicious relationship begun by Nixon and Kissinger.

Vance's view was less clear-cut. It conformed to the prudential wisdom of international politics. Statesmen must not confuse means and ends. One country cannot define the destiny of another. It can seek to influence conduct, but rarely can define a regime's policy or save it. Apart from the East-West settlement at the end of World War II (Communist rule in Eastern Europe) there was little evidence that in many revolutions and changes of regime either superpower had much influence. Vance believed it would have been wrong for the United States to go any further in support of the Shah. His position was morally and politically consistent,[22] because he experienced the same reservation about overturning the Somoza regime.

Another dictator whose fall that same year (1979) was destined to complicate life for the Carter administration was Anastasio Somoza Debayle, whose family had ruled Nicaragua for forty years. The Carter human rights campaign was not directed against any particular regime. When denouncing state terrorism before the Organization of American States in June 1977, Vance was stating a principle and, to the extent that he was thinking of Latin American regimes, those of Chile and Argentina were in his mind. But the administration's emphasis upon human rights was bound to worry the dictatorships ruling in Nicaragua, El Salvador, and Guatemala as well. That, following half a century of support for repression, an administration should talk about human rights was surely enough to heighten tension.

The question is why the United States failed to move sooner and more effectively to disengage itself from Somoza and similar rulers in Central America where, as in the case of the Shah, their power appeared to depend so completely upon American support. By the time the Carter administration took office, several countries of Central America were in a state of near revolution. Economic benefits had accrued only to the wealthy landowning class from the sale of beef, coffee, and other crops on the international market. Educated and professional classes were fed up with oligarchic and military rule, electoral fraud, and corruption. The Catholic Church was openly in opposition. The problem for the Carter administration was how to make changes before it was too late.[23]

Nowhere was the crisis more acute than in Nicaragua, where broad opposition to the rule of Somoza had been gathering. Somoza had manipulated the country for his own welfare and that of his supporters, economic and military. Business and professional classes had organized the Union Democratica de Liberacion, led by the editor of *La Prensa*, Pedro Joaquin Chamorro. In the countryside and among the poor, the Frente Sandinista de Liberacion National (FSLN) sought Somoza's overthrow by violence. Somoza used the revolutionary activity of the Sandinistas to justify repression. Clearly, he would have to go. The logic of the need for change and the desirability of insuring a moderate outcome were intellectually recognized. But the reflexive belief that it was somehow wrong to push out a sitting government, or to "intervene," or to try and shape internal political events in another country, all effectively weakened the will and coherence of strategy. The fear of betraying one's own principles was quite strong. Thus the administration's conflicting concepts cross-sterilized each other.[24]

The administration's initial response in Nicaragua was to offer inducements to Somoza to get him to open up the system. The Christopher interagency group recommended a restriction of economic and military aid—a mere slap on the wrist at a time when Somoza had crushed the Sandinistas and reestablished sufficient domestic order that he could avoid the grossest violations of human rights. In August 1977, over Vance's opposition, Carter sent Somoza a letter expressing satisfaction with the steps to improve human rights. The letter took notice that the dictatorship was to admit members of the Inter-American Commission on Human Rights and in addition consider an amnesty for political prisoners, together with electoral reform. Then in January 1978, when Somoza's henchmen were linked to the assassination of Joaquin Chamorro, support for the Sandinistas revived. Ensuing months saw widespread repression and systematic killings by Somoza's National Guard, and it became clear that Somoza would have to go.

Whether any action by the United States—from reducing the meat quota and International Monetary Fund credits to telling Somoza outright that he had to resign—would have worked is difficult to say. Any forceful move would have meant standing up to Somoza's supporters in Congress. Vance needed to get Somoza out if the Sandinistas were not to be the principal beneficiaries. He felt it was wrong to bring about the fall of a country's government, even with the intent of producing a more popular government.[25] It is easy to scoff at such scruples, noting that the United States had seldom observed them when it was a question of getting rid of a left-wing regime. Somoza, sensing this tentativeness, gained the confidence to proceed in the most ruthless way in dealing with his opposition.

The beginning of violent insurrection in Nicaragua in September 1978 convinced the administration to act. Vance now believed that Somoza's removal was a sine qua non for avoiding violence that would consume centrist elements and bring the Sandinistas to power. By contrast, it was in Somoza's interest to eliminate the moderate opposition so as to justify his rule as a bulwark against Marxists and revolutionaries.

The United States led a three-nation mediation team to Nicaragua in early October. The State Department's Bureau of Inter-American Affairs, headed by Viron Vaky, hoped Somoza would withdraw in favor of centrist forces of the United Opposition Front. The team sought to secure Somoza's resignation. However, Vance was unable to secure Carter's support for all-out pressure. The team rejected a United Opposition Front proposal that Somoza and his brother, who commanded the National Guard, resign.[26]

The United Opposition Front next submitted a proposal that would have left Somoza's Liberal Party in power and merely reorganized the National Guard under incumbent officers. This proposal split the centrist opposition, many members bolting to the Sandinistas.[27] Over the State Department's opposition the White House then allowed the mediation team to pick up a proposal by Somoza's Liberal Party to hold a plebiscite. Somoza in the end rejected the presence of international observers that the team deemed necessary.

Preoccupied with Iran, Vance seems to have been unable or unwilling to obtain President Carter's support for the bureau of Inter-American Affairs recommendation for ousting Somoza.

Doubtless he shared the concern that the political costs of forcing Somoza out were too great. Unfortunately the failure of the mediation team brought centrists to believe that Somoza would never leave of his own free will. Both sides took advantage of the mediation effort to rearm and soon were ready for a showdown. Nicaragua thereupon turned into a holocaust, as Sandinistas and the National Guard fought street by street, town by town.

Washington called for help from the Organization of American States. Vance considered it important that the United States maintain a multilateral approach. An OAS resolution would lay the basis for continued multilateral monitoring to keep the internal Nicaraguan situation as "pluralistic" as possible. His initial recommendation had been that the United States seek guidance of the OAS. He did not specify an "OAS presence" or peacekeeping force. It was clear that an OAS presence was synonymous with U.S. intervention, and Latin American governments were no longer willing to endorse such a solution. Several governments also had recognized the belligerent status of the Sandinistas. Hostility toward Somoza and impatience with U.S. maneuvering was widespread.[28]

Desperation now drove the White House to do what it could to prevent a Sandinista takeover, and the result was what Vance and the other advisers had predicted: the other governments rejected the call upon the OAS to send a peacekeeping force and establish a broadly based regime. The OAS resolution asked for immediate replacement of Somoza.[29] The best Vance could do was to word the resolution to say that the Sandinistas could not sweep away the rights of other parties, meaning Nicaraguan businessmen and the centrists. The administration's accusation of Cuban support for the Sandinistas, and refusal to break diplomatic relations with Somoza, strengthened Sandinista antipathy. Somoza's stubborn effort to crush the revolutionary forces, which now included virtually all Nicaraguans, came to nothing. The dictator resigned on July 7, 1979.

Given its history of support for Somoza and, later, of his moderate opposition, the Carter administration could not expect to prevent the Sandinista regime from moving in a pro-Cuban and pro-Soviet direction. Nevertheless the administration asked Congress for sizable economic aid.[30] The argument, with which Vance agreed, that the outcome of the Nicaraguan revolution would depend in part on how the United States reacted was of course sound. The hope that practical considerations might constrain radical impulses within the new regime was to prove illusory in light of the Sandinista leaders' ideological position and their experience with the U.S. role in Nicaragua. Critics of the Carter administration were now in a position to exploit the charge that support for human rights and diplomacy had led only to appeasement—when in fact neither had had much impact on the final result.[31] The public was not prepared to recognize the way in which developments over many years had trapped the United States in Central America, or appreciate the merits of working with other countries to contain an awkward revolution.

The memory of the hideous aftermath of the overthrow and assassination of Diem was still fresh in Vance's mind. When America removes a foreign leader it assumes responsibility for subsequent events. Whoever comes to power in the wake of an American imposed coup or resignation is identified as an American creation. Improvement though it might be to rid Nicaragua of Somoza, Vance was dubious about the responsibility that America would be assuming, not to mention the possible backlash from right-wing forces in the Congress.

## CHAPTER FOURTEEN

# The Demise of SALT
# (Part Three)

Despite the fall of the Shah and the success of the Sandinistas in Nicaragua, Vance's diplomacy continued to make headway. The Guadeloupe economic summit showed European relations essentially sound. The Israeli-Egyptian peace treaty, signed in Washington March 26, 1979, ended thirty years of hostility. The SALT II agreement would come in June. On June 28, the House of Representatives would vote, 350 to 37, in favor of sanctions against the Rhodesian government, effective until such time as it agreed to accept the principle of "one-man, one-vote." The Soviets and Cubans had bogged themselves down in Ethiopia, and far more powerful South African forces in Namibia balanced what little significance Soviet-Cuban presence represented in Angola. Vance had contained Soviet influence by diplomatic means. All this hardly justified the epithet of critics that the Carter administration had reduced foreign policy to a "stagnant and irresolute state."[1]

The centerpiece of Vance's diplomacy was of course SALT II. Vance and his associates had negotiated a SALT treaty according to the most exacting standards and in scrupulous consultation with the Senate. They had set their sights on an agreement that would stabilize nuclear arsenals of the superpowers and provide for the security of allies. The undertaking—a balanced and verifiable treaty that would win senatorial acceptance—had taken longer than expected but results justified the effort.

Vance later wrote that SALT "enjoyed a powerful base of popular support which could be mobilized." Actually public support was apathetic. Of those citizens who had heard or read about SALT (58 percent) less than a third said they would like to see the treaty ratified (10 percent said no, 18 percent had no opinion).[2] A Roper poll (December 1978) was downright disconcerting. Only a third of respondents could identify the parties to the negotiation and when informed that SALT involved the United States and the Soviet Union, only a bare majority identified SALT as an attempt to limit long-range nuclear weapons.

Understanding of the President's foreign policy was at an all-time low. Carter arrived in office when the reaction against Vietnam had crested. The succeeding two years witnessed a remarkable reversal in public attitudes. The plurality that had favored détente in the early 1970s had now become a plurality expressing distrust of the Russians; the pluralities against more military spending had now become pluralities in its favor. In 1969 half of the American public thought too much was being spent; by 1976 that had dropped to a third, while those favoring the same level or higher had increased to more than half.

Concern over Soviet behavior, and its effect on support for SALT, appeared in questions asked in public opinion polls in June 1978. One dealt with trusting the Soviets to comply with a new treaty. Almost two thirds of respondents felt that the Soviet Union would not "live up to its share," while only one fifth felt it would. Just over half felt the United States should "get tougher," and less than a third indicated the United States should "try harder to relax tensions." Brzezinski argued that unless the administration showed toughness it would risk support for SALT. Vance knew that any more so-called toughness would kill off the Soviet commitment to SALT. Actually, Carter had shown toughness commensurate with Soviet actions in Africa and with maintaining Soviet-American relations. Except for Iran, the diplomatic balance was as much in America's favor as in the Soviets'. No American soldiers had died in a futile intervention.

The administration was fighting a losing battle in its effort to educate. The chastened post-Vietnam mood was yielding to reassertiveness. (There was no evidence, however, that the public would support a new war.) The perception that the Carter administration was letting the Soviets get away with something in Africa had been reinforced by Carter's rhetoric, and frustration about foreign affairs was taking the form of either blaming the Russians or the administration. Despite détente or perhaps because of overselling it, no strong constituency desired to improve relations with the Soviet Union. Certainly nothing matched the reviving emotional opposition to rapprochement with "aggressive, repressive and atheistic totalitarianism."[3] Under these circumstances the Carter Administration's performance, whether or not adequate in terms of its goals, was susceptible to accusation that it had failed. The American public did not understand the fact that in order to negotiate with the Soviets, leeway must be allowed for compromises.

The ignorance and volatility of public opinion assisted the coalition of interests opposed to SALT and to Carter's foreign policy generally. Organizations like the American Security Council and its Coalition for Peace through Strength, as well as the Committee on the Present Danger, desired to defeat SALT and reassert military superiority. The American Security Council was a throwback to the "Red on the Map" propagandists of the 1950s, who had seen Soviet communism advancing insidiously across the globe. It enlisted 162 congressmen in the Coalition for Peace through Strength and reached community opinion through widely disseminated films. The Committee on the Present Danger, founded a few days after Carter's election, was headed by Nitze and Eugene Rostow. Its executive board eventually included Lane Kirkland, president of the AFL-CIO, and other labor leaders. Nitze's record of service under several administrations, including a period as SALT I negotiator, gave him authority. He and Rostow were both Democrats and their sponsorship of an organization opposed to détente and determined to defeat SALT reflected the schism in the Democratic Party as a result of Vietnam. Repudiation of the war and breakup of the Cold War consensus had divided the Democratic Party, with Carter the heir of the anti-Cold War tendency. The losers were seeking vindication.

To both the America Security Council and the Committee on the Present Danger—dominated by retired officers, defense industrialists, and defense intellectuals—everything the Carter Administration stood for was anathema. To demonstrate that SALT II would fail to protect American security, that it was in fact "an act of appeasement," to use Senator Jackson's term, prompted its enemies to concoct a wholly specious argument. Developed by Nitze for the Committee on the Present Danger, it contended that any treaty with the Kremlin was worthless unless backed by American superiority; that under SALT II the Soviets had the capacity to knock out 90 percent of U.S. land-based missiles in a pre-emptive strike; that being untrustworthy and out for world domination, the Kremlin would not hesitate to use that advantage either for diplomatic blackmail or, in event of a showdown, to strike first; that an American President confronted by such a threat or such an action, and knowing that an American act of nuclear retaliation would wipe out civilization, would not respond. The Soviets, being more ruthless than Americans and prepared to write off millions of their own people, would not hesitate to use this scenario. Accepting parity or essential equivalence with the Soviets (Nitze argued it was not equivalence), SALT II placed the free world at risk.[4] So the argument ran.

Apart from the fact that such a scenario assumed Soviet willingness to risk an attack that might not succeed, and would not foreclose a launch-on-warning retaliatory strike by thousands of warheads from U.S. submarines, bombers, and aircraft ringing the Soviet Union, the scenario posited a willingness to risk confrontation at a level that the Soviets had not approached since the Cuban missile crisis.[5]

To appreciate the distortion promulgated by these SALT II critics, it might help to set it against the remarks of Warner Schilling, a dispassionate analyst, who began by asking if the United States would "find it easier to deny the Soviets any expectation of victory or advantage *within* the constraints of a SALT agreement *or without them.*" American policy makers needed to recognize that particulars of any SALT agreement were the product of so much intra and intergovernmental bargaining that SALT II might strike any observer as less than satisfactory. Since SALT II did not prevent the United States from deploying weapons it considered necessary for its strategy of countervailing power, and since the treaty bound the Soviet threat in important dimensions, Schilling concluded that the United States would probably find it cheaper to insure military parity within the agreement than without.[6]

Far from stimulating American policy to anything but a return to the Cold War, the anti-SALT supporters were prescribing paralysis for America's leadership. European allies were altogether in favor of SALT and warned of loss of confidence in America if SALT failed. A move to scuttle SALT would be, in one observer's words, an example of "all those things critics of the negotiating process fear and warn against. It would be a failure of will, a failure of nerve, and, most important, a failure of imagination the United States can ill afford."[7]

The other group opposed to détente and the SALT treaty, principally on moral grounds, was composed of neo-conservative intellectuals who had turned against détente partly because of the immorality of dealing with a totalitarian state and partly because of Soviet support for Israel's Arab enemies. While the American Israel Public Affairs Committee and other such organizations avoided positions on national security issues, they contributed to a political environment unfavorable to improved relations with the Soviet Union. This was especially true of *Commentary*, which became one of the main vehicles for articles attacking Vance's policy.[8] The frequent theme in *Commentary* and in the writings of its editor Norman Podhoretz was that Carter-Vance policy amounted to appeasement. The message that ran through much of the anti-détente, anti-Carter writing and that was especially marked in *Commentary* posited a crisis of belief and will brought on by the Vietnam War, and insisted that unless we overcame it we were doomed.

In the absence of any major constituency committed to improved relations with the Soviet Union, the power of opponents was bound to be enormous. The prestige of the many opponents of SALT ensured that their views would have a wide hearing. Ever more sensational accounts of America's decline and vulnerability by anti-détente defense intellectuals, picked up by columnists, augured ill.[9]

The treaty's fate depended on the Senate, where its friends hoped that extremists would not be able to dictate policy. No treaty could secure a two-thirds vote without some willingness on the part of the opposition to keep an open mind.[10] Treaties invariably had to count upon bipartisan support, but bipartisanship was no longer something Presidents could count on. Republican leader Senator Baker declared the treaty too important not to be a partisan issue and justified opposition on the grounds that negotiation had not been linked to Soviet behavior in other areas.[11] He promised to avoid politics, but had given the signal. Throughout the debate he made clear that he was against the treaty.

To make matters worse, Hatfield, Proxmire, and McGovern (joined by Adlai Stevenson, Jr.) announced opposition because the treaty did not go far enough toward slowing the arms race and would permit the Defense Department to proceed with new weapons.[12] Finally and perhaps most decisive, Senator John Glenn warned against accepting the treaty on the basis of statements of faith in Soviet intentions and called verification inadequate. He proposed that the Soviet Union allow American aircraft to fly along the Soviet border and allow monitoring devices inside the Soviet Union.[13]

Carter addressed a joint session of Congress and did everything possible to convince listeners that he had not based the treaty on trust of the Kremlin or illusions about détente. It reduced the danger of nuclear war by codifying the East-West balance, preserved the option to build an additional system to maintain the strategic balance, and made Soviet-American competition "safer and more predictable, with clear rules and verifiable limits where otherwise there would be no rules and there would be no limits." He pointed out how much greater both in numbers and power Soviet and American arsenals would become if the treaty did not pass.[14]

When the Foreign Relations Committee opened hearings, Vance was first to testify, and pointed out that SALT was one area of Soviet-American relations where it was in the national interest to reach agreement, regardless of Soviet activities in other areas. SALT II was not a favor we were conferring on the Soviets. He acknowledged it was not possible to end competition or eliminate antagonism and the determination of each side to meet its security needs. Nor could we force the Soviet Union to disband its heavy missile force, because that was their strategic defense, just as the triad— land, sea, and air—was America's. The treaty improved strategic stability while reserving the proposed MX system, with its ten warheads and multiple aim points, which the joint chiefs considered would maintain the triad's land-based leg. It gave America's allies reassurance. It reduced the chance of proliferation. If other states were not to develop nuclear weapons the United States and Soviet Union had to set an example.[15]

Vance warned that rejection would cause "severe worsening" of relations in the decade ahead and a "terribly severe blow" to NATO.[16] He acknowledged that it could not end the race, but it would maintain equivalence and open the way for future agreement. He appealed to such moderates as Senator Stevenson, that it would stabilize the arms race and make possible reductions.[17] To meet the criticism of those who argued that the Soviet Union by about 1982 would be able to destroy almost all of the 1,054 U.S. land-based missiles in a surprise attack, he argued that it could not as readily destroy the MX in a mobile mode and would maintain "essential equivalence" in the sense that, like the Soviet SS-18s and 19s, the MX could destroy hard sites in the Soviet Union.

Vance found it disturbing that the treaty's opponents dismissed support by NATO allies as political. In a speech at the Harvard commencement Chancellor Schmidt warned that failure to ratify could result in a return to the Cold War. President Giscard later joined Schmidt.[18] SALT II played a part in European willingness to accept intermediate-range nuclear weapons. Acceptability of Pershing IIs and land-based cruise missiles depended upon ratification, after which the whole question of theater weapons, including Soviet SS-20s, would become part of the so-called SALT III follow-on. Vance had every reason to regret the Senate's obsessive concern with military aspects of SALT II at the expense of larger strategic and political considerations.

The opposition mounted every argument against the treaty. As Vance pointed out, the MX system, whatever its basing, depended on SALT II's ratification. Otherwise the Soviets could so "fractionate" their heavy missiles as to target even "dummy" silos.[19] But Nitze and General Rowny said it increased Soviet warheads, ignoring the "cap" it placed upon fractionation. The issue of ratification became a vehicle for critics seeking to force the administration to increase defense spending. The administration had begun to move in that direction, but it was not enough. Senator Nunn declared that "no foreseeable arms control agreement can be an adequate substitute," ignoring the fact that no one intended the treaty to be a substitute.[20] Witnesses from the Committee on the Present Danger and their Senate allies attacked the treaty as undermining America's will to defend itself and as a prescription for appeasement. "They believed that SALT negotiations were a drug and that you had to destroy the soporific potion before it was administered."[21] The unwillingness of the CIA director Turner to agree categorically that loss of the Iranian monitoring stations had not impaired U.S. ability to verify Soviet compliance opened a Pandora's box. Defense Secretary Brown testified that the Iranian loss could be offset within a year and that nothing the Soviets might do would tilt the balance without our knowing in time. But he could not undo the damage done by Turner's scrupulous conscience. Just as the administration had hoped to meet Senator Jackson's terms, it counted upon Kissinger's endorsement. Instead Kissinger hedged and conditioned his support in a carefully staged presentation.[22]

By Senator Cranston's tally, at the end of August 1979, forty senators favored the treaty, twenty opposed, with forty undecided. For the twenty opponents, the treaty constituted appeasement based on the misbegotten belief that the United States could trust the Soviet Union. How could a President conduct policy in the face of such obsessions? It is all very well to say in retrospect that Carter had doomed the treaty because he had not earned respect or that his ineptitude had lost the mandate of heaven. But was it ever intended under the Constitution that the Senate should escape its obligation? Recognition that political extremes may perform a positive function did not mean that they should "dictate national policies in an area as crucial as the U.S.–Soviet relationship." This was what was occurring. The need for a great nation to be wise and consistent was being sacrificed to the hysteria of a minority whose opposition rarely included realistic and serious alternatives.[23] It is difficult, after the fact, to appreciate the extent to which conviction in the Senate that any dealings with the Soviet Union were treasonous, added to fear of wavering Democrats that they might appear "soft on the Soviets," mortgaged the fate of SALT II.

As for the undecideds, many were intent on cover excuses to avoid a positive vote that might prove controversial. This attitude prompted many undecideds to look to Glenn or Nunn for reasons to postpone the vote. Nunn argued for holding off until defense expenditures were raised. Glenn claimed (two years later he reversed himself) that he could not in conscience support a treaty without perfect verification. As a contemporary observer wrote, "Arms control agreements do not have to be perfect in order to be useful. Our choice is not between imperfect and perfect arms-control agreements; it is between imperfect agreements and none at all. Verifiability is only one desirable quality, and not the most essential, of a satisfactory agreement. If we subject our diplomacy to arbitrary rules—for example, to the rule that all agreements must be verifiable—we are subordinating human judgment to technology and making arms control subservient to the gathering of intelligence."[24]

By the time of the Secretary's final testimony, the administration was mildly hopeful that it could educate the public and win undecided senators by promises to increase defense spending. Unfortunately, the reported presence late in August of a Soviet combat brigade in Cuba brought on overtones of crisis.

There had been intelligence as early as 1978 that Soviet military presence in Cuba was growing. The reported arrival of eighteen or twenty crated MIG-23 aircraft on board Russian ships in late April had been leaked to newspaper columnists. Were the MIG-23s capable of carrying nuclear bombs? That would violate the 1962 agreement by which Russia agreed not to introduce nuclear or offensive weapons. Vance raised the issue with Dobrynin, warning that it would jeopardize acceptance of SALT II. Carter warned the Soviets in a televised news conference on November 30. Intelligence subsequently demonstrated that the MIG-23 was not equipped to carry nuclear bombs.

In the summer of 1979 the National Security Agency detected Soviet reference to military training forces in Cuba as a brigade. Carter ordered surveillance to determine the character of the unit. Meanwhile, as early as July 17, 1979, Senator Stone, a Florida Democrat with a strong Cuban constituency, had picked up information of a combat force. Asked by Stone to confirm or deny, the administration hedged. Senator Church, chairman of the Foreign Relations Committee, succeeded in winning from his committee, Stone dissenting, a statement of "no evidence of any substantial increase in the size of the Soviet military presence in Cuba."[25] Vance wrote Stone that besides the Soviet training unit "our intelligence does not warrant the conclusion that there are other significant Soviet forces in Cuba." On August 17 reconnaissance satellites took photographs of a Soviet force maneuvering with tanks. Vance was now authorized to make representations to the Soviet government while downplaying its significance. Again a leak occurred. Discussion led him to decide that Hodding Carter should make brief reference to it; meanwhile Undersecretary David Newsom would inform congressional leaders. Church, vacationing in Idaho and facing a fight for his Senate seat, was informed. Church called Vance to ask whether he or the President intended to announce the finding. Hearing only that the administration intended to take it up with the Russians and unable to reach the President vacationing in Georgia, Church announced the existence of the brigade and said it must be removed.[26] "There is no likelihood whatever," he said, "that the Senate will ratify the SALT treaty as long as Russian combat troops remain in Cuba." Vance managed to get this threat rescinded the next day, but the damage had been done.

In what he later regretted as an error, Vance announced that the brigade's presence was "a very serious matter" contrary to "long-held American policies." While it did not pose a threat, as had Russian missiles in 1962, he would "not be satisfied with maintenance of the status quo." In the absence of information as to what the brigade amounted to, Vance had put himself and the administration on a limb. Soviet reaction was rapid. Called back from the deathbed of his father in Moscow, Dobrynin met Vance on September 10, and four times in the next two weeks. On September 24 and 27, Vance met Gromyko in New York. The Soviets refused to consider the demand for the brigade's withdrawal or even for a cosmetic concession.[27] American intelligence subsequently revealed that while the brigade did not seem to have any training purpose, neither did it appear to have any airlift or sealift capabilities.

The Soviets apparently had interpreted the hullabaloo over the brigade as an American attempt to extract concessions on SALT II. The administration had taken a position that it found hard to prove. The Soviets became indignant, and overreacted. To save the treaty, Carter went on television on October 1, to announce unilateral U.S. measures to neutralize the brigade. But Russell Long, an influential member of the Senate, meanwhile had changed his vote to oppose

SALT II, giving as his reason Soviet "bad faith." By the end of October there was no evidence that as many as 65 senators would vote for SALT II. In Moscow the positive climate that followed the signing of the accords had begun to dissipate.

Vance's effort to reject linkage and insulate SALT was always at the mercy of such an incident, however marginal or specious. His SALT strategy made a heavy claim upon American tolerance for Soviet competition. He supported the administration's plan to increase defense spending and develop the MX as a counterpart to seeing SALT II ratified. He was convinced that neither superpower could tilt the balance against the other except at risk of nuclear war, and that his diplomacy in the Middle East, Africa, and NATO took the measure of Soviet competition. Vance's Soviet strategy rested upon a presumption that the substance of power is more important than the shadow, that American and NATO power guaranteed Western security. The American people and their representatives were prisoners of another image that took the shadow for reality. Only one strategy found acceptance—hostility dominated by a zero-sum view. It made everything Vance was seeking vulnerable to even the slightest upset.[28]

The SALT II treaty was reported out of committee by a narrow margin—9 to 6—on November 9, 1979. The final blow to ratification came in December with the Soviet invasion of Afghanistan.[29]

# CHAPTER FIFTEEN

# End of the Line

Once the Shah decided not to take up the administration's offer to provide him with a California sanctuary, and went to Egypt and then Morocco, Carter and Vance decided it would be unwise to admit him to the United States. The situation in Iran had become radical because of the competition for power (and survival) among religious and revolutionary factions, and much more anti-American. Events in Iran conformed to the aphorism attributed to Louis XIV, "Après moi le déluge." For eight or nine months Iran was drenched in blood as the regime revenged itself on enemies and as factions that had made the revolution found themselves, with the Shah gone, at drawn daggers. This was no blessing for America, because new enemies had to be found if the Ayatollah Khomeini was to maintain himself, and to this end the United States was increasingly the "great Satan." Just as the Committee of Public Safety found a response to revolution in 1792 only when Europe presented the French with a common enemy, so Carter and Vance appeared to recognize that America was the candidate for such a role. An effort to normalize relations made little headway. Iran refused to accept Walter Cutler as ambassador, obliging Washington to send L. Bruce Laingen as chargé d'affaires.

Vance and Carter were aware, or so it seemed, that to admit the Shah to the United States would be taken in Iran as further humiliation, evidence that Washington might once again, as in 1953, restore the Shah to the Peacock Throne. They rejected pressure from David Rockefeller and Henry Kissinger that their friend the Shah be admitted. But Brzezinski believed that we owed it to the Shah to admit him on the ground that not to do so "would be a sign of weakness . . . would be a signal to the world that the U.S. is a fair-weather friend."[1] Here again was the long-standing penchant of identifying policy with a leader and not with the country or with the people. Critics often accuse the State Department of clientelism—favoring the regime in power—but Kissinger and Brzezinski were proposing to make a deposed tyrant a protected favorite of the American government, despite warnings from Teheran.

The President and Vance, Hamilton Jordan has written, saw the Shah's problem differently: "As long as there is a country where the Shah can live safely, and comfortably, the President reasoned, it makes no sense to bring him here and destroy whatever slim chance we have of rebuilding a relationship with Iran."[2] It boiled down to a choice, Carter observed, "between the Shah's preference as to where he lives and the interests of our country."[3] Pressure thereupon mounted. Kissinger "openly expressed his disgust with the administration's failure to provide asylum for the Shah to political friends and members of the press" and hinted none too subtly that he would condition his support for SALT on the response.[4] Senator Baker took to the floor of the Upper House in April 1979, urging admission, and Senator Percy and Majority Leader Byrd too argued that Americans "cannot turn our back on a man who was our friend."[5] Here was total insensitivity to the hatred that thirty years of support for the Shah had engendered and no appreciation of the fact that America's power to control events was no longer as great as it once had been.

When Vance raised the issue with the President on October 19, 1979, he had changed his position. The Shah's physician, the prominent New York pathologist Dr. Benjamin Kean, was urging entry because the royal patient needed treatment available only in the United States. Kean said it would be preferable to have the Shah treated in the United States. The alternative, treating him in Mexico City, was not made clear to Vance.[6] The secretary felt as a matter of principle that the Shah should be admitted. "The President argued alone against allowing the Shah in."[7] For once the President's political instincts were sound and those of his advisers, including Vance, faulty. The risk of admitting the Shah should have been recognized. By securing the promise of Prime Minister Bazargan and Foreign Minister Yazdi that their government would protect the embassy, the U.S. Government only succeeded in giving Khomeini opportunity to reassert his authority by calling for new demonstrations against the great Satan.[8]

Early in October, Chargé Laingen had warned that "real hostility toward the Shah continues, and . . . the augmented influence of the clerics might mean an even worse reaction than would have been the case a few months ago, if we were to admit the Shah—even for humanitarian reasons."[9] On the eve of admission both Laingen and the Iranian desk officer on mission to Teheran, Henry Precht, were emphatic in stating that admission was likely to provoke an outburst.

The result unfolded as ineluctably as Carter had forecast. Vance arrived back from the funeral of South Korean President Park (murdered by his chief of intelligence) at 8:30 P.M. on Saturday, November 3. Shortly after 3 A.M. Sunday his special assistant, Arnold Raphael, awakened him with news that a mob had placed the Teheran embassy under siege and was about to take it.

For the next fourteen months Iran held the administration hostage. Thousands upon thousands of State Department hours were consumed in securing the hostages' release. The spectacle turned the country upside down, destroying whatever chance Carter had of being reelected.

Once it became clear that the Iranian government was not going to free the hostages, who were at the mercy of their captors, Vance saw no recourse but to work for release by economic sanctions and diplomacy: "a judgment that U.S. military action would only stimulate the Shi'ite fervor for martyrdom [was] the major reason behind an early decision to use patient diplomacy and concentrated international pressure rather than force."[10] The President set his course by the conviction that he must maintain honor and national interest while working to get the hostages out. For the first five months Vance sought to press Iran. Policy then developed along two courses—a diplomatic, managed by Vance and Christopher, and a military, designed to rescue the hostages, pushed by Brzezinski.[11]

Vance decided that short of putting the hostages on trial and threatening to execute them, nothing justified force and everything called for diplomacy. As Carter later stated, "First we decided that should a public trial of the hostages occur, we would interrupt *all* commerce with Iran as soon as the first trial began" and contingency plans looked to a blockade of the entrances to Iranian seaports. "We also had to meet the more serious problem of physical punishment or execution of the hostages," and the administration prepared a plan "to make a direct military attack on Iran." It considered, and dropped, a proposed rescue mission, following a pessimistic report by the joint chiefs of staff, only to take it up a month later on a highly secret basis.

The President directed Vance to employ all avenues of negotiation while building pressure through the allies and the United Nations to bring home the cost to Iran of holding the hostages. On November 9, Carter ordered a boycott on military parts and equipment and on November 13 a boycott of Iranian oil. When, in early hours of November 14, Iran announced it would withdraw all deposits from American banks, a call from the Secretary of the Treasury at 4:00 A.M. awakened Vance, and at 8:10 A.M. Carter signed papers freezing Iranian assets—an effective move because the pinch caused by economic chaos and need to get access to assets finally brought the hostages' release. Meanwhile, the hostages appeared safe, although that hardly appeased Americans having their captivity reviewed on television night after night. To add to the administration's trouble, and any lingering hope Vance may have had of seeing SALT II ratified, Soviet forces invaded Afghanistan.

The Soviet invasion of Afghanistan on December 25 raised all kinds of questions about an American policy of restraint and nonconfrontation. Left and right argued over nuclear war and foreign relations in the context of how expansionist, how untrustworthy, how evil the Soviets were. Vance was endeavoring to break out of that closed system. He did not believe Afghanistan invalidated his approach. He believed it was as much the responsibility of a Secretary of State to avoid putting America at the mercy of unrelenting Cold War and the potentiality of nuclear war as to maintain security for America and its allies. Just as he had protested too strongly in the case of the Cuban brigade, he later rejected the charge that he took a soft line on Afghanistan to protect SALT II, pointing out that it was because of the need to defend SALT that he had reacted (and overreacted) to word of a Soviet brigade in Cuba. He argued that because he wanted to see SALT ratified "he would have been eager to prevent the Soviets from invading Afghanistan, since such an act of aggression would be apt to sabotage relations with Congress."[12]

American policy had treated Afghanistan as part of the Soviet sphere long before Vance became secretary, and so it seemed as if whatever political convolutions occurred in Kabul they were of no real concern to the United States. As long as Iran buffered American interests in the Persian Gulf, few Americans in or out of government worried about Afghanistan. Until 1978 a non-Marxist regime had ruled Afghanistan, led by Mohammed Daoud, who had given indication of reasserting Afghanistan's independence by developing ties with neighbors—Iran and Pakistan—but without challenging the ties to Moscow or abandoning nonaligned status within the U.N. Daoud, a populist who publicly eschewed socialism and carried the banner of unreconstructed Islam, gradually assumed the status of an autocrat and squeezed out those Afghan Communists, who afforded Moscow part of its influence.[13] Another source of Soviet influence came from the presence of 3,500 Soviet advisers, many attached to the Afghan Army. The two American ambassadors who served in Afghanistan under Daoud—Robert Neumann and Theodore Eliot— agree that Daoud's policy shifts "did not lead to his overthrow, because the changes did not alter the fact that Russia still had much more influence in Afghanistan than any other country."[14] Possibly Daoud's shift to the right in conjunction with U.S. moves in the region (a proposal as early as 1977 to establish some form of rapid-deployment infrastructure) may have aroused Soviet suspicion.

The cause of Daoud's overthrow in April 1978, however, seems to have been the determination of Marxist rivals to carry out a coup d'état, which they did. Headed by Nur Mohammed Taraki, leader of the Khalq faction of the Marxist movement (as opposed to the Parcham faction led by Babrak Karmal) and his even more doctrinaire associate Hafizullah Amin, the new regime soon made known its pro-Soviet alignment. Despite mounting evidence of the new regime's pro-Communist orientation, and its unpopularity, the Carter administration pursued an accommodationist approach, continuing aid and withholding judgment, on the basis that there was nothing much it could do. The tragic death of the American ambassador Adolph Dubs, seized by foes of the regime and killed in a shoot-out with Afghan security forces (with Soviet advisers present), prompted a sharp reaction from the administration, Carter accusing the Soviets of involvement in the bungling that caused Dubs' death.

Within months the Taraki regime's attempt to impose Marxist doctrines upon the Afghan people had produced insurrection. "As the rebellion grew and the regime showed itself less and less able to repress it, the Soviets were forced to increase their role in the conflict . . . until by the middle of November 1979, there were perhaps as many as 4,500 advisers in the country."[15] Having committed themselves to the support of a Marxist regime, the Kremlin was unlikely to tolerate its collapse.

What happened next was not what the Kremlin expected. Concerned with hostility that the ambitious and ideologically zealous Amin was arousing, the Kremlin leadership apparently advised Taraki, on a visit to Moscow in September 1979, to get rid of Amin. Instead, when Taraki arrived back in Kabul and invited Amin to the People's Palace, the residence of the president, a wild West shoot-out occurred in which Taraki was killed. Having turned the tables on Moscow, Amin could scarely have felt himself secure from a Soviet plot.

Instead of taking public cognizance of Afghan events, Vance left the problem to his spokesman, Hodding Carter. Afterward he acknowledged responsibility for not having been more outspoken:

> In looking back, I think we should have expressed our concerns more sharply at the time of the April coup that brought Taraki to power. There were reasons why we did not protest more vigorously. Although there was little question that the Taraki government would make itself responsive to Moscow, there was room for doubt about whether the Soviets had planned the coup or were involved in its execution. And there was reason to think the strong Afghan nationalism of Taraki, and even more of Hafizullah Amin, might keep Afghanistan from becoming a Soviet satellite. . . . We concluded that our interests would best be served by letting Afghanistan continue its traditional balancing act between East and West. The United States

had few resources in the area and historically we had held the view that our vital interests were not involved there. Moreover, our friends in the region had adopted a wait-and-see attitude. There was no disposition on their part to add to the instability by supporting opponents of the Marxists in Kabul. Although we were contacted from time to time about coup plots, my advice was that we not get involved. 16

Even Brzezinski acknowledges that he had approved of a re-strained approach to the Communist coup, for the same reason as Vance. "What could we have done? It was an internal coup, there was no evidence of Soviet involvement, and hence there was no ground for an American protest."17

Less excusable was Vance's failure to anticipate the invasion and warn Moscow that if the massing of troops on the Afghan border was a prelude to intervention, the damage to Soviet-American relations would be incalculable. Although concerned not to worsen a rela-tionship under stress, there was precedent to assume that the Soviets might use the troops, and to warn both the Kremlin and the American public. Whether it would have made any difference is problematic. Afghanistan was to all intents and purposes a Soviet satellite, a condition precedent for the Kremlin not to hesitate at drastic action. The Brezhnev Doctrine had codified the principle that if any client regime was threatened the Soviet Union had the duty to intervene. The insecurity that the Kremlin felt for its borders and empire dictated the conclusion that no Communist state, particularly a border state, could reverse its status. Brezhnev subsequently expressed the view that the State Department should have recognized as gospel: "The revolutionary process in Afghani-stan is irreversible."18 And even if such reasons did not exist for intervention, the American disarray attendant upon the fall of the Shah and seizure of the hostages, together with Soviet uncertainty about its own strategic stake in the region, would have been incentive enough to take action. The propensity of great powers to assert themselves in their own spheres was only distinguished in the Soviet case by the ruthlessness of the means employed.

After Vance had detected the buildup of troops, he informed Dobrynin privately that "if this was a move toward Soviet military intervention, it would be seen as a very grave matter by the United

States."[19] This and other statements did not achieve their purpose, perhaps because they were "discussions" and not "warnings" or because they came late. Intelligence analysts could not give (nor should they have been expected to) a conclusion as to what the massing of forces might portend. But apart from whether it would have deterred the Soviet Union, Vance or Carter should have protested publicly, if for no other reason than to protect the administration from the American public. It was important, as Vance admitted, to warn the Kremlin against sabotaging relations with Congress and defeating any hope of SALT, although the shift to the right emerging from the SALT hearings may have been a factor in shifting the political climate in Moscow.

One can only say it was a mistake for Vance or Carter not to have warned the Soviets. It seems likely that Vance let his wish be father to the thought that nothing serious would occur. The very facts that should have heightened his concern about events in Afghanistan— the fall of the Shah and seizure of the hostages—was so all-consuming that it was difficult to focus on any other issue.[20]

Soviet invasion of Afghanistan did not validate the argument of people who argued that Soviet strategy is expansionist world-wide. It did more to justify Vance's position that Soviet behavior was cautious and determined by security and status as a superpower, and that to moderate such behavior America's policy ought to combine military readiness and diplomacy. In the Soviet hierarchy of values, security of borderlands is an obsession, just as the presence of Castro and Sandinista regimes in their security zone obsessed Americans. Afghanistan illustrated the unpredictability or, perhaps more accurately, the predictability of Soviet behavior in acting with ruthless concern for security, where temptation existed and risk and cost appeared low. Nothing demonstrated or perhaps even suggested that had Vance made linkage and the threat of military intervention in the Horn of Africa a condition of policy vis-à-vis the Soviet Union he would have deterred the Kremlin. One could as well argue that suspicion over the developing Sino-American link and its implications for Soviet interests in Southwest Asia had prompted the invasion.

The invasion appeared to Americans as a challenge. The subheading to an article by Hedrick Smith in the *New York Times Magazine* of January 27, 1980, read, "By Invading Afghanistan, Moscow Challenged the United States on New and Untested Terrain." Smith argued that the invasion represented what Brzezinski called "a qualitatively new step with disturbing implications that reach far beyond the Soviet effort to stamp out Islamic tribal rebellion . . . and to protect its client government in Kabul." In fact there was no evidence that the invasion represented more than that, but given its aggressive character and coming at a time and in a region where U.S. interests seemed to be crumbling, the invasion elicited the strongest American reaction. That Vance had projected a view of Soviet competition limited to indirect intervention, unlikely to upset the world or regional balance, prompted what may have been overreaction. At a moment when the Soviet military buildup of the previous decade was rising to ominous levels, and with the Carter defense buildup in its initial stage, the invasion reinforced the argument that the Soviets had determined to exploit their power on a world scale. Nor could any American administration overlook the fact that it had occurred in a region important to American interests. Brzezinski argued that a tougher anti-Soviet line earlier might have deterred the Soviets from invading. Vance argued that had relations not been deteriorating, and the danger of American-Chinese-NATO encirclement not growing, the Soviet Union might have been more cautious. Neither hypothesis is demonstrable since we have no access to the reasoning behind the Soviet decision. Whatever Vance's hope that the Soviet Union would exercise restraint, failure to do so gave the administration no choice but to move closer to the view of Brzezinski.[21] The administration adopted a strategy of making the invasion as costly as possible. Although the administration had been toughening its line all through 1979, Carter incautiously spoke as if the Soviet action came as a revelation, strengthening the public view that he had never understood the Soviets.[22] His response was to ask the Senate to delay action on SALT II, followed by curtailment of grain shipments, cutoffs in technology transfer, and abrogation of Soviet fishing privileges in American waters. He followed with an all-out campaign to mobilize the United Nations to denounce Soviet intervention and demand the immediate, unconditional, and total withdrawal of Soviet forces (carried by a General Assembly vote of 104 to 18 on January 14, 1980).

Carter set out his strongest expression of determination to respond to Soviet action and draw the line against further moves in the State of the Union message, reaffirming the 1959 security agreement with Pakistan, which proposed military facilities in the Persian Gulf and called for a rapid-deployment force. More to the point, Carter declared that "an attempt by an outside force to gain control of the Persian Gulf region will be regarded as an assault on the vital interests of the United States" and "will be repelled by any means necessary, including military force."[23]

Afghanistan hence took on major importance. On January 4, 1980, just as Secretary of Defense Brown was leaving for China, Carter reversed a decision and decided that Brown should offer nonlethal military equipment and high technology items. Vance would have liked to maintain a balance in relations, as a hedge against confrontation and Cold War, also as a bridge to improvement after the damage from Afghanistan had been repaired or run its course. If the policy was intended to punish the Soviet Union for aggression, then it ought to have been to some purpose and not wasted in anger. But when Vance asked approval to meet with Gromyko in March 1980, Carter refused. Vance's views were no longer as acceptable. By contrast, Brzezinski could hardly contain his ebullience that Afghanistan had vindicated his views and headed the administration in the right direction, "as a result of the Soviet threat to the Persian Gulf."[24]

It soon became evident that our NATO allies were not prepared to follow the new American policy 100 percent. Upon return from seeing Schmidt on February 20, Vance reported that the chancellor's "earlier determination to stand fast with us was melting as quickly as snow in a late Rhineland winter."[25] On January 9, Schmidt had declared that the Federal Republic would not follow the United States in retaliating against Moscow for aggression.[26] And that was not the worst. Under pressure from the collapse of SALT II and West German concern not to lose détente, in spite of Afghanistan, Schmidt was beginning to renege on his commitment of December 1979 to deploy NATO medium-range theater nuclear weapons, with or without Dutch and Belgian acceptance.

For Vance all these problems were soon to be over. From the time the Iranian mob seized the hostages he had held that the best way to secure their release would be economic sanctions and diplomacy. Until the invasion of Afghanistan, military options to secure the hostages, or retaliation against the Iranians, had been under consideration, but according to Brzezinski the invasion of Afghanistan "made it more important to mobilize Islamic opinion against the Soviets" and avoid anything that "might split Islamic opposition to Soviet expansionism."[27] Goaded by his sense of responsibility and by the desire to avoid the resort to force, Vance and associates, particularly Christopher, pursued the diplomatic approach. Unfortunately, neither the intercession of Waldheim, with an offer to give Iranian complaints against the United States an international hearing after release of the hostages, nor economic sanctions against Iran instituted with reluctant backing of our allies, nor the subsequent abortive effort by some of Khomeini's underlings to have the government take control of the hostages, availed.

All diplomatic initiatives to free the hostages having momentarily failed, Carter met with advisers at Camp David on March 22, 1980, to discuss the issue. Vance again opposed force, including a blockade or mining, as long as the hostages were unharmed. He was thinking not only of the hostages but of American interest in not forcing Iran to turn to the Soviets, or worsening U.S.–Islamic relations. He believed that the situation inside Iran would make negotiation possible, that as time passed the likelihood of physical harm diminished. The President was testy. This was not the advice to satisfy him or his advisers, including Brzezinski. His reelection depended on some stroke that would free him from the appearance of indecisiveness and weakness.

Brzezinski had conceived of a rescue mission if hostages were killed or about to be killed. Now the administration undertook it for other reasons: to respond to public pressure and to get Carter reelected. Brzezinski reported that in the three weeks after the March 22 meeting a decision crystallized, with Vance kept in the dark, to go forward with the rescue mission. The final act had to wait until Vance was off the scene. Brzezinski sped it along on April 10 by giving Carter a memorandum entitled "Getting the Hostages Free," in which he argued that negotiating had come to an end and direct action must ensue.[28]

On Thursday, April 10, Vance and his wife left for a weekend in

Florida, and next day a meeting of the National Security Council decided on a rescue mission. Christopher attended as acting secretary but without briefing he found himself isolated in arguments against it. Christopher told Vance of the decision taken in his absence. Stunned and angry, he saw the President the following morning and received the chance to present his views to another meeting of the National Security Council. Preparing his notes, Vance was convinced of the folly of the proposed mission, principally because of the risk—not only to the hostages but the two hundred newsmen and other Americans in Teheran, and because of the potential for damage to the country's diplomatic relations and the promise of progress in gaining release by diplomatic means. His appeal to reconsider the decision was of no avail. The self-deceiving and self-serving argument was made that the only alternative to a rescue mission would be a naval blockade, which would deliver Iran to the Soviets.[29]

The following day, while Carter was reviewing military details of the mission and passing on Brzezinski's stalwart advice that he, Carter, unlike Kennedy at the time of the Bay of Pigs, not "interfere with operational decisions," Vance pondered his decision to resign. After talking it over with his wife and several aides, including Christopher and Linowitz, he made up his mind he could not stay. Even if the mission worked, which he doubted, it would put him in an impossible position. If asked to testify he would have to give his reasons for opposing the mission. He informed Carter, who in his curiously insensitive way urged him to stay because he could explain later that he had opposed the mission.

Monday, April 21, Vance handed Carter his resignation to take effect after the mission. On April 24 he was presiding over a meeting in the Situation Room when Carter asked him to come to the Oval Office. There he learned, with initial relief, that the mission had aborted, only to have the President learn of an accident at the site that killed several men. Over the next days Vance waited for Carter to appoint his replacement. Undaunted, Carter instructed Brzezinski to plan another mission, in Brzezinski's words "a simpler mission, based on the injection of a large force into Tehran, combined with the seizure of a larger airfield."[30] The first mission, Brzezinski believed, had created public pressure for a large-scale military action. Vance was relieved to be free of a situation where he could not, in conscience, any longer usefully serve. On Sunday, April 27, the President told him he had chosen Senator Edmund Muskie as his replacement, rather than Christopher, whom Vance had recommended. On the morning of the twenty-eighth Vance met with Carter to receive the President's letter accepting his resignation.[31]

# CHAPTER SIXTEEN

# Conclusion

Carter won election to the presidency while the American public was still reacting to the eight-year nightmare of Vietnam and had not absorbed the meaning of Kissinger's policy of détente—that the United States no longer enjoyed nuclear superiority, no longer possessed the power to impose its will upon the noncommunist world. People had admired Kissinger because he maintained the illusion of America's primacy. He and Nixon had conceded nuclear parity to the Soviet Union and recognized Red China in *Realpolitik* fashion, giving the Russians equality in hope that they might cooperate in maintaining the status quo. His apparent realism gave pride of place to the superpower relationship and had for its corollary the presumption that the rest of the world would be subordinate. It wrote off Eastern Europe as part of the Soviet sphere, while it managed much of the rest of the world according to American preferences. By arranging this apparent transformation with fanfare, the Republican administration had succeeded in disarming its critics. Only individuals like Senator Jackson, who for ideological or strategic reasons did not believe the United States should concede anything to the Soviets, became Kissinger's critics.

The lesson that Americans had to learn, and that Kissinger's world view precluded, was that neither superpower could any longer dominate others short of military intervention, and then only at great cost, as the Soviets are learning in Afghanistan.

Carter proposed to apply this lesson. He proposed to move beyond realism and restore what he described as idealism. He thus attempted, in a sense, to go beyond Kissinger. The transformation in America's relations with the Communist powers was to extend to the rest of the world. Far from fearing change, he welcomed it. America had more to offer the rest of the world than did the Soviet Union. In an increasingly complex and interdependent world, in which all nations were becoming assertive, the United States had more concerns than just the Soviet Union. The U.S. must change its reputation for supporting authoritarian regimes just because they were anticommunist. Instead of polarizing conflict along East-West lines, especially in the Third World, where people struggled for freedom or at least for relief from poverty and exploitation, the United States would not only tolerate change but help it along.

If this was Carter's prescription for policy, it was even more Vance's.[1] A man of compassion, he saw a world of suffering human beings whose lot he sought to ameliorate. He also saw a world ever more dangerous. This was no personal matter. Governments owed it to their peoples to do something. The potential for tragedy through nuclear war was no abstraction.

Second, Vance shared Carter's belief that not only would foreign policy be better but it would be more effective if free from anticommunism. The latter restriction was not only unncessary; it was stultifying. America would be no less secure if it acted on the premise that the Soviet Union was another great power—more insecure in its legitimacy, hence more repressive, imbued by a messianic doctrine that shaped its view of the universe and made it dogmatic, nonetheless subject to the same risks and costs as other powers. Its situation was no more roseate than America's, less if one considered that it faced NATO in the West and China in the East. It was in American interest to temper the competition where most dangerous, in nuclear armaments.

Third, Vance shared Carter's confidence that change was not so dangerous to America's interest as to require uncritical support of abhorrent regimes simply because they professed anticommunism.

Fourth, he shared Carter's view that the United States should not link a nuclear arms agreement to Soviet activities in other areas. As Deputy Secretary of Defense he had watched the nation commit itself to a war in Vietnam to contain China, only to have Nixon and Kissinger woo Moscow and Beijing to contain Hanoi. The experience had given him a healthy contempt for geopolitical conceptualizing with its delusive abstractions like credibility and linkage.

If Carter brought courage and inspiration to this view or approach, Vance brought the other indispensable ingredient—skill and tenacity as an analyst and negotiator. The spirit and challenge of the law may imbue its practitioners with confidence in the capacity to bring conflicting parties to understand their interests, and in Vance's case this matched a marvelous capacity for analysis and negotiation. Experience as a lawyer in a large firm made it possible for him to inspire colleagues without browbeating them. Instead of the degradation of diplomacy by strategy and military thinking, he restored the diplomatic art to American statecraft.

Vance sought to put America's influence to work. He resisted the simplistic strategy of imposing an East-West dimension on every issue and sought instead to apply U.S. influence to resolution of conflict rather than polarizing each situation. He wanted to combine containment with diplomacy and negotiation. Kissinger showed how little he had learned from Vietnam, Africa, and the Middle East when he declared that "The United States must show that it is capable of rewarding a friend or penalizing an opponent. It must be made clear . . . that our allies benefit from association with us and our enemies suffer. . . . for a great power it is the prerequisite, indeed the definition of an effective foreign policy." What happened when allies paid no attention to wishes and still had to be rewarded or at least tolerated, when costs of punishing an enemy exceeded any rational advantage and might in fact be highly counterproductive? The Secretary of State of 1977–1980 could point to the determination of other countries, including Communist states, not to become pawns of the Soviet Union. This determination had prevented Soviet expansion and aided in preserving a political balance between the superpowers. Without abandoning containment, he argued against exaggerating the issue of Soviet expansionism. Third World states had both the interest and ability to resist, and where a government like Castro's let itself be used, it had lost credibility. Opposition by other nations to the Soviet Union, Vance argued, relieved the U.S. of viewing every gain in Soviet influence as a threat to America's credibility and made for a more rational process in determining whether and where to exert influence.

Vance's course was straightforward enough that one would have thought anyone could have understood it: to use diplomacy and not be confrontational. Hence emphasis upon SALT II, and projected deployment of theater nuclear forces in Europe subject to a new round of negotiation. Hence the Panama Canal treaty to remove an issue before it ruined Latin American relations. Hence defusing tensions in the Near East by working toward an Israel-Egypt treaty. Compared with Soviet intrusion into Ethiopia, the Camp David Conference made a far larger contribution to regional security. Vance applied the same principle in southern Africa, successfully in Zimbabwe, in promising fashion in Namibia. He was less successful in Iran and Nicaragua.

There was a great deal to be said for Carter-Vance policy, and certainly in comparison to the limitations, even the shallowness, of Nixon-Kissinger and Ford-Kissinger diplomacy. And yet Carter and Vance necessarily would have trouble in making rationality—which they were advancing under the form of idealism—prevail. While it was true that most challenges and threats no longer came from the Soviet Union, it was also true that they came from trends in world politics that resisted governability by power in any form. The inclination of European allies to persist in détente; the ungovernable condition of many if not most Third World countries; the inability of traditional and even nationalist elites to establish legitimacy in the face of explosive and corrosive economic and social change; the inadequacy of economic aid and private investment that once gave America leverage but no longer sufficed; regional wars assisted by foreign armaments and nationalist and religious ambitions—all these presented Washington with new and intractable problems. It was no longer the heroic time of the high Cold War. In most parts of the world America appeared as part of the problem, not part of the solution.

Substituting diplomacy for military power also involved the risk of appearing weak and indecisive.[2] Even the prestidigitator Kissinger had not been able to conceal from the American public the fact that détente did not mean the end of Soviet-American competition. Nor did it conceal his costly failure to get out of Vietnam with honor. So much more difficult was to be the Carter administration's struggle to explain a policy designed to achieve complex objectives without the traditional anti-Soviet accompaniment. Vance's diplomacy also could not serve or be tolerated by constituencies basically hostile to the Soviet Union—superpatriots, the military-industrial complex, the Israeli lobby. It was terribly vulnerable to upsets not caused by policies but by events over which the administration had little control, such as the collapse of the Shah's regime in Iran or the Soviet invasion of Afghanistan. Having eschewed a zero-sum, confrontational style, the administration was more vulnerable to the charge that it lacked toughness and will. The spectacle of the embassy hostages was symbolic of the frustration and powerlessness against which many Americans felt a need to react. Such a mood was fatal to Vance's diplomacy for securing their release.

The President, too, was a source of danger, as well as support, to Vance's diplomacy. He was not always ready to accept the contradictions and inconsistencies of idealism. When faced with the Kremlin's activity in Africa and his own belief that good will ought to be reciprocated, Carter succumbed to Brzezinski's argument that Soviet behavior constituted an unacceptable breach of détente. Instead of attempting to educate Americans to contradictions, Carter resorted to finger-pointing. He attempted to come down on both sides, offering the Soviets a choice between good relations or confrontation but not attempting to convince the American public that Soviet gains, such as they were, did not threaten the United States. The denouement might well be said to have been inevitable. Carter, his presidency and reelection at stake, felt driven to break out of the confines of reason with the rescue mission.

Carter and Vance both were subject, one should add, to the incoherence that has been built into the American political system and makes management of anything but the most stereotyped Cold War policy extremely difficult. No other parliamentary system makes foreign policy so difficult. No administration that gets its way all the time in foreign policy does so without deception and chicanery, usually with demagogic appeal. Vance tried to conduct an open policy and paid the price.

Not only did Congress become much more active in imparting incoherence and inconsistency, but during the Carter-Vance years the media created an impression of incoherence whenever contradictions appeared. Story after story reported an alleged departure from some mythical consistency, and the media dwelt upon these contradictions as though they were proofs of weakness.[3] Historically the media had embellished the performance of some administrations and denigrated that of others. In 1977–1980 the public did not accept the idea of complexity and ambiguity and looked for simple explanations. The media were quick to provide them.

Moreover, in economic concerns, domestic and foreign, the Carter administration was having no easy time—and the economic problems of the era exacerbated all diplomatic problems. President Carter inherited an economy that was experiencing the first full effects of stagflation. For two and a half years he managed to avoid the Charybdis of inflation and the Scylla of unemployment. Fear of recession and unemployment alternated every six or seven months with fear of inflation. The energy program he introduced in April 1977 stalled in Congress, where its implications for oil company profits and for the consumer caused problems.[4] In 1978 inflation in the United States, fueled by the OPEC oil hike of that year, began to arouse anger in other countries. In spite of attracting foreign investment capital, record trade and current account deficits made the dollar decline steadily. Although the overburdening of the American economy was due in part to the costs associated with defending Europe, Carter's proposal that West Germany and Japan share the burden of stimulating the international economy elicited a blunt rejection.[5] In the summer of 1979 domestic tensions over economic policy came into the open. Secretary of the Treasury Michael Blumenthal resigned, along with Energy Secretary James Schlesinger and Secretary of Health, Education and Welfare Joseph Califano. This wholesale dismissal of cabinet members reflected a crisis in the American economy for which there was no longer any easy answer. In the early summer of 1979 came gasoline shortages caused by breakdown of the Iranian economy and reduction in oil from the Persian Gulf. All these were circumstances bound to devastate any Democratic administration.

Within the administration Vance's style provided strength and integrity. He was a secure person who did not feel driven to self-promotion. He conducted himself according to the old-fashioned code by which one person respected another. In the face of Brzezinski's machinations, this probably saved the administration the spectacle of crude power rivalry. Had he gone out of his way to sharpen the conflict, as Brzezinski's memoirs reveal that Brzezinski did, the administration's reputation for incoherence would have been much greater. It was a point of honor with Vance not to play Brzezinski's game. This may have given the impression that the latter's views were in the ascendancy long before that actually became the case. Vance's largest problem was to counter Carter's inclination to give in to Brzezinski, to take the easy way out. It says something for Carter, however, that he generally supported Vance.

In contrast to Carter, Vance's relations with Congress were rather good. He was better liked than Brzezinski.[6] Congressmen never questioned that he was out there doing his best. He had access to the congressional leadership on a personal basis. This of course did not mean he could carry them on every issue. He did not attempt to articulate his policies the way Kissinger did for Ford. And in an administration that lacked good communicators, he assigned much of the responsibility for dealing with the media to Hodding Carter.

Within the department Vance appeared distant, but he had strong backing. He enhanced the department's spirit of professional pride by restoring diplomacy to its place of primacy in the conduct of foreign policy. He also spend considerable time on new foreign service legislation. He was seen as a human being, both in his relations with subordinates and in the effort he and his wife made to entertain ambassadors of lesser countries.

Vance's stewardship marked an effort to avoid return to the Cold War. He dealt with the Soviet Union as another great power with which it was in America's interest to lessen conflict. For the United States to impose an East-West dimension on every challenge was costly and unnecessary. His defeats were honorable, the result of forces beyond his control. His outlook was hopeful but not utopian, his skills appropriate to the task the President set. Above all he believed, as did his distinguished predecessor Dean Acheson, that mankind need not and must not be a passive victim of fate.

# Notes

## Chapter One

1. William H. Harbaugh, *Lawyer's Lawyer: The Life of John W. Davis* (New York: Oxford University Press, 1973), p. 390.

2. *Year Book 1935: The Kent School.*

3. *Yale Yearbook,* Class of 1939.

4. Erwin O. Smigel, *The Wall Street Lawyer* (Glencoe, Ill.: The Free Press, 1964), p. 37.

5. Ibid.

6. Ibid., p. 105.

7. Richard Powell, *The Philadelphian* (New York: Scribners, 1956), p. 75.

8. Thomas Thatcher himself, together with Dean Acheson, prepared the brief on the editorial page of the *New York Times* arguing that Roosevelt had legal authority to transfer destroyers to Britain (in the summer of 1940). David S. McLellan, *Dean Acheson: The State Department Years* (New York: Dodd, Mead, 1976), p. 40.

9. *Congressional Quarterly,* August 18–24, 1962, p. 1418.

10. Another area of reform initiated by Vance was in ending racial discrimination in housing around military bases. "Cy came up with the idea that the military should establish the rule that no personnel would accept housing that was restricted to whites." Interview with Robert S. McNamara, Washington, October 7, 1983.

11. U.S. Army oral history interview with Vance, April 15, 1976, p. 52, Army War College, Carlisle Barracks, Penn. See also Larry Berman, *Planning a Tragedy: The Americanization of the War in Vietnam* (New York: W.W. Norton, 1982).

12. Paul M. Kattenburg, *The Vietnam Trauma in American Foreign Policy: 1945–1975* (New Brunswick: Transaction Books, 1980), p. 126.

13. Oral history interview, March 9, 1970, p. 3, Lyndon B. Johnson Library, Austin, Tex. Vance observed that like others he could not help but be disappointed by Johnson's decision to exploit the Christmas 1965 bombing pause by making such a public show of sending peace emissaries to meetings with foreign leaders instead of striving for confidential contacts with Hanoi. Ibid., p. 15.

14. Berman, *Planning a Tragedy,* p. 123.

15. Townsend Hoopes, *The Limits of Intervention* (New York: David McKay, 1969), p. 50.

16. Vance, oral history interview, Johnson Library, p. 6: "in hitting targets in the north you had to consider that you were going to affect third countries such as the Russians and the Chinese, and the whole problem of world opinion was different when you were dealing with the bombing of North Vietnam as opposed to . . . South Vietnam." Ibid., p. 8.

17. Hoopes, *The Limits of Intervention,* p. 50. Hoopes enlarged upon this in an interview with the author. Washington, D.C., September 23, 1983.

18. Oral history interview, Johnson Library, p. 19. "Despite the talk about the briefing for the March 1968 meeting being far more pessimistic, I don't think they were any more pessimistic as compared to previous information I had received. . . . Johnson's reaction to the change of view was not explosive—the vast majority at the meeting felt that the course of the war had to be changed." Ibid., pp. 19–20.

## Chapter Two

1. William J. Jorden, *Panama Odyssey* (Austin: University of Texas Press, 1984), pp. 68–69.
2. Interview by author with Vance, October 14, 1983. See Abraham F. Lowenthal, *The Dominican Intervention* (Cambridge, Mass.: Harvard University Press, 1972).
3. Oral history interview, Johnson Library, November 3, 1969.
4. Ibid. Also "Final Report of Cyrus R. Vance, Special Assistant to the Secretary of Defense, Concerning the Detroit Riots, July 23–August 2, 1967," p. 7.
5. Thomas Ehrlich, *Cyprus: 1958–1967* (New York: Oxford University Press, 1974); Nancy Crenshaw, *The Cyprus Revolt: An Account of the Struggle for Union with Greece* (London: Allen and Unwin, 1978); Theodore Coulombis, *The United States, Greece and Turkey: The Troubled Triangle* (New York: Praeger, 1983).
6. Chester Cooper, *The Lost Crusade* (New York: Dodd, Mead, 1970), p. 396.
7. Ibid., pp. 400–401. At a press conference on July 31, Johnson told reporters that 30,000 North Vietnamese had moved into South Vietnam during that month, indicating his distrust of an unconditional bombing halt.
8. Warren I. Cohen, *Dean Rusk* (Totowa, N.J.: Cooper Square, 1980), p. 313.
9. Ibid., pp. 403–4.
10. Oral history interview with Vance, March 9, 1970, Johnson Library.
11. Ibid. Throughout these months, Vance relates, the Russian embassy clarified for the North Vietnamese what was being said and what the U.S. expected. Vance worked through the deputy chief of mission in the Soviet embassy in Paris and in Washington through Ambassador Dobrynin.
12. Ibid., p. 28. Vance argues that Thieu learned in October that the National Liberation Front would be represented and that Premier Thieu had said he was "prepared to go forward." Ibid., p. 30. It is possible that Mrs. Claire L. Chennault had passed the word to Thieu that he would get a better deal under Nixon.
13. Chester Cooper, *The Lost Crusade*, p. 407.

## Chapter Three

1. Ole R. Holsti and James N. Rosenau, *American Leadership in World Affairs: Vietnam and the Breakdown of Consensus* (London: Allen and Unwin, 1984). Michael Mandelbaum and William Schneider, "The New Internationalisms" in *Eagle Entangled: U.S. Foreign Policy in a Complex World*, edited by K. A. Dye, D. Rothchild, and R. Lieber (New York: Longman, 1979), pp. 34–90.
2. John Lewis Gaddis, *Strategies of Containment* (New York: Oxford University Press, 1982). See Gaddis's "The Rise, Fall and Future of Détente," *Foreign Affairs* 62 (1983–84): 4; also Stanley Hoffmann, *Primacy or World Order: American Foreign Policy since the Cold War* (New York: McGraw-Hill, 1978); Seyom Brown, *Faces of Power* (New York: Columbia University Press, 1983).
3. Brown, *Faces of Power*, p. 456.
4. William Lee Miller, *Yankee from Georgia* (New York: Times Books, 1978), p. 122.
5. Ibid.
6. Ibid.
7. Miller, *Yankee from Georgia*, p. 146.

8. Zbigniew Brzezinski, *Power and Principle: Memoirs of the National Security Adviser, 1977–1981* (New York: Farrar, Strauss and Giroux, 1983), p. 12.

9. Bruce Russett and Elizabeth Hanson, *Interest and Ideology: The Foreign Policy Beliefs of American Businessmen* (San Francisco: W.H. Freeman, 1975).

10. Cyrus Vance, *Hard Choices: Critical Years in American Foreign Policy* (New York: Simon & Schuster, 1983), p. 446.

11. Ibid., p. 29.

12. Ibid., p. 34.

13. James E. Carter, "A Foreign Policy Based on America's Essential Character," address at the University of Notre Dame, May 22, 1977.


## Chapter Four

1. Brzezinski, *Power and Principle*, p. 11. Asked by Carter to evaluate Vance for the post of Secretary of State, Califano told the President-elect that "Vance was not only brilliant but has as much integrity as any person I've ever met." Carter responded "I don't doubt it, but is he tough enough to be Secretary of State?" Joseph A. Califano, Jr., *Governing America* (New York: Simon & Schuster, 1981), p. 15.

2. Individuals who worked with Vance in the Department of State write that in the interim between leaving the Defense Department and returning as Secretary of State, he moved from safe centrist positions to a more liberal line, "from being a man whose career had defined the center to someone who would take the point position on controversial issues he cared about." I.M. Destler, Leslie Gelb, and Anthony Lake, *Our Own Worst Enemy: The Unmaking of American Foreign Policy* (New York: Simon & Schuster, 1984), p. 96.

3. Jimmy Carter, *Keeping the Faith* (New York: Bantam Books, 1982). Brzezinski argued the opposite: "Carter's was perhaps formally the most centralized of all in the postwar era." Ibid., pp. 74, 513. On the complexity of organizing the presidency for foreign policy, see Alexander L. George, *Presidential Desicion-making in Foreign Policy* (Boulder, Colo.: Westview Press, 1980), pp. 159–62; Robert Hunter, *Presidential Control of Foreign Policy: Management or Mishap?* (New York: Praeger, 1982); Leslie Gelb, "Why Not the State Department?", *Washington Quarterly*, Special Supplement, Autumn 1980, pp. 25–40.

4. Carter's personality adversely affected the organization and management of his advisory system, for which see such articles as by his former speechwriter Fallows, "The Passionless Presidency," *Atlantic Monthly*, May 1977, pp. 33–46. For Brzezinski's emergence as a challenger to Vance, see Don Bonafede, "Brzezinski Stepping Out of His Backstage Role," *National Journal*, October 15, 1977, p. 1598; Elizabeth Drew, "A Reporter at Large: Brzezinski," *New Yorker*, May 1978.

5. Alexander L. George, *Presidential Decision-making in Foreign Policy*, p. 160.

6. Vance, *Hard Choices*, p. 37.

7. Todman, a black, went as ambassador to Spain because of his opposition to the human rights emphasis.

8. Interview with Anthony Lake, September 30, 1983.

9. Ibid. Seyom Brown, *The Faces of Power*, p. 459, relates much the same thing: "Cyrus Vance, although as aware of the geopolitical realities as any of Carter's advisers, and hardly indifferent to Soviet expansionism . . . differed with Brzezinski over the best means of limiting it . . ."

10. James E. Carter, "The U.S.–Soviet Relationship," Dept. of State *Bulletin*, August 15, 1977, pp. 193–97.

11. James E. Carter, "A Foreign Policy Based on America's Essential Character," (address made at the commencement exercises of Notre Dame University, South Bend, Ind., May 22, 1977). Dept. of State *Bulletin*, June 13, 1977, pp. 621–25.

12. David P. Calleo, "American Power in a New World Economy," in William Becker and Samuel Wells, Jr., eds., *Economics and World Power* (New York: Columbia University Press, 1984), p. 395.

13. Zbigniew Brzezinski, *Between Two Ages: America's Role in the Technetronic Era* (New York: Viking, 1970).

14. Ibid., p. 175.

15. Ibid., pp. 159–64, 282.

16. Ibid., p. 190.

17. Ibid., p. 191.

18. Ibid., p. 285.

19. Cyrus Vance, "Meeting the Challenges of a Changing World," Dept. of State *Bulletin*, June 1979, pp. 16–19.

20. Zbigniew Brzezinski, "American Policy and Global Change," address to the Trilateral Commission, Bonn, October 25, 1977.

21. Brzezinski, *Power and Principle*, p. 149.

22. Ibid.

23. Ibid., p. 165.

## Chapter Five

1. William D. Jackson, "Soviet Images of the United States as Nuclear Adversary, 1969–1979," *World Politics* 33 (1981): 614–38. Of SALT I, Brezhnev declared: "It is impossible to overestimate the significance of the fact that the U.S. and the Soviet Union have agreed to act in a manner to rule out nuclear war." Jackson writes, "In the period following the Vladivostok summit, bifurcation in Soviet thinking about SALT and U.S. strategic policy remained much in evidence." It is unlikely that Brezhnev would have fended off criticism from within the military and from those opposed to détente "if he had not believed that agreement on the Vladivostok accord was imminent." Peter M.E. Volten, *Brezhnev's Peace Program: A Study of Soviet Domestic Political Process and Power* (Boulder, Colo.: Westview Press, 1982), p. 115, is even more sweeping and categorical in assessment of the extent to which Brezhnev had been forced to go out on a limb to secure Politburo support for the Vladivostok accord. Vladivostok was the high point of Brezhnev's struggle to maintain détente. "Brezhnev badly needed to pick up momentum in foreign policy . . . controversies in the Soviet polity had reached the point where American credibility regarding détente had become a yardstick by which to measure Brezhnev's policy."

2. Volten, note 1 supra, pp. 120, 131. Volten contends that SALT "greatly politicized strategic matters."

3. Ibid., p. 120.

4. *Pravda*, June 14, 1975, quoted in William D. Jackson, "Soviet Images," p. 629.

5. Thomas N. Bjorkman and Thomas J. Zamostny, "Soviet Politics and Strategy Toward the West," *World Politics* 36, no. 2 (January 1984): 203.

6. The revised CIA estimates first appeared on September 20, 1983, in testimony by the deputy director for intelligence, Robert Gates, in open testimony. They are

from the CIA briefing paper, "USSR: Economic Trends and Policy Developments," September 14, pp. 8–11. See U.S. Congress, *Hearings Before the Joint Economic Committee on the Allocation of Resources in the Soviet Union and China, 1983* (Washington, D.C.: Government Printing Office, 1983), pp. 19–20.

7. "By contrast Vance had immense respect for Kissinger, and that respect seemed almost completely undiluted by envy . . . Vance was also a profoundly secure individual. He knew his strengths of which 'stick-to-itiveness' was one." Strobe Talbott, *Endgame* (New York: Harper & Row, 1980), p. 79.

8 Ibid., p. 58.

9 Ibid., p. 59. Brzezinski, too, appears to have argued that Nixon, Ford and Kissinger had "gone down a blind alley on the Soviet turf and it was time to get back on our own." The only question Warnke raised was that if the new proposals failed "we'll be criticized for retreating." Ibid., pp. 58–59.

10. Brzezinski, *Power and Principle*, p. 160.

11. Ibid. The tone of Brzezinski's diary is one of satisfaction that the Soviet Union is on the spot. On March 30 he confided that "if the American public stands fast and we do not get clobbered with the SALT issue, I think we can really put a lot of pressure on the Soviets. . . . I can well imagine that the Soviets feel in many respects hemmed in. However, all of that could begin to collapse if any of our colleagues begins to act weak-kneed and starts urging that we make concessions to the Soviets." Ibid., p. 162. It is difficult to imagine a Soviet specialist who could have been so far off in judgment of Soviet psychology as Brzezinski on this occasion.

12. Brzezinski, *Power and Principle*, p. 162.

13. Ibid.

14. Quoted in Talbott, *Endgame*, pp. 78–79.

15. Ibid., pp. 90–91.

16. Brzezinski, *Power and Principle*, p. 167.

17. Ibid.

18. Ibid.

19. The subsequent Soviet decision to set a limit of 820 for land-based, MIRVed ICBMs was a concession to the United States. Ibid., p. 169. But so was the agreement to impose an identical ceiling on MIRVed ICBMs for both sides of 1,200 while "in effect allowing the United States an additional free 120 ALCM-carrying heavy bombers through the imposition of a joint ceiling of 1,320 on all MIRVed ICBMs and ALCM-carrying bombers combined, since the Soviets did not have ALCM-carrying heavy bombers." Ibid., p. 20. The history of bargaining chips is not a happy one. All too often the chip does not get bargained away but becomes part of the nuclear arsenal.

## Chapter Six

1. Vance, *Hard Choices*, p. 85.

2. Brzezinski, *Power and Principle*, pp. 178–79.

3. Ibid., p. 181.

4. Ibid.

5. Interview with David Aaron, October 10, 1983.

6. Brzezinski, *Power and Principle*, p. 185.

## Chapter Seven

1. Ishaq I. Chanayen and Alden H. Voth, *The Kissinger Legacy: American Middle East Policy* (New York: Praeger, 1984), pp. 173–74.
2. Vance, *Hard Choices*, p. 448.
3. Ibid, p. 164.
4. Interview with Harold Saunders, December 20, 1983. Alfred Atherton writes that "Secretary of State Cyrus Vance made a determined effort to obtain PLO agreement to a formula designed to satisfy the requirements of our 1975 agreement with Israel and thus make possible the opening of a direct U.S.–Palestinian dialogue. The PLO leadership, divided over how to respond, failed in the end to seize the Vance opening." "Arabs, Israelis and Americans," *Foreign Affairs*, Summer 1984, p. 1203.
5. Carter's espousal of the right of Palestinian self-determination in the course of a "town meeting" (a randomly chosen locality where the President answered questions from local citizens) may have helped tip the scales against the Labor government, inasmuch as in Israel "self-determination" was a code word for a Palestinian state opposed by a majority of Israelis. It seems more likely that support for the Labor party eroded for other reasons, including the revelation that Yitzhak Rabin's wife had maintained an account in a Washington bank in contravention of the Israeli law requiring accounts of all nationals to be in shekels. Election of the Likud coalition headed by Begin marked a dramatic shift and a challenge to Vance's hopes. Begin's election marked the breakthrough into Israeli politics of a new and powerful sector of Israeli society—that of the Oriental Jews who had come from minority status in Arab lands and hence did not have the same tolerance for the Palestinians as did Israelis of European origin. Shlomo Swiski, "The Oriental Jews in Israel: Why Many Tilted toward Begin," *Dissent*, Winter 1984, pp. 77–91.
6. Ofira Seliktar, "The New Zionism," *Foreign Policy* 51 (Summer 1983): 118–38.
7. Vance, *Hard Choices*, p. 181. Begin made no secret of his intention to pursue the annexation of the West Bank. Alarmed by Carter's severity on the settlement issue Begin's advisers asked him what he planned to do. "Begin replied that he would build the settlements as planned. The Americans, he predicted, would turn cold for six months, then they would revert to normal." Eric Silver, *Begin, the Haunted Prophet* (New York: Random House, 1984), p. 168.
8. Ibid., p. 182.
9. Carter, *Keeping Faith*, p. 286.
10. Interview with William Quandt, September 19, 1983. "Vance never made threats or blustered. There was a strong, firm streak in Vance that did not keep him from speaking his mind even to the Israelis. For example, he thought we ought to be tougher on the Israelis—we ought to cut aid in the amount equal to what was going into the West Bank settlements and he meant it. He did not hesitate to assert his views, however strongly held, but not in a belligerent manner."
11. Ismail Fahmy, *Negotiating for Peace in the Middle East* (Baltimore: Johns Hopkins University Press, 1983), p. 215.
12. Ibid., p. 213.
13. Andrew Pierre, "Beyond the Plane Package: Arms and Politics in the Middle East," *International Security* 3, no. 1 (Summer 1978): 148.
14. Vance, *Hard Choices*, p. 213.
15. Ibid., p. 214.
16. Silver, *Begin, the Haunted Prophet*, p. 189.
17. Ibid.

## Chapter Eight

1. For a comparison between the human rights record of the Nixon-Kissinger and Carter administrations, see Lars Schoultz, *Human Rights and United States Policy toward Latin America* (Princeton, N.J.: Princeton University Press, 1981), pp. 109–34.

2. Abraham F. Lowenthal, "Jimmy Carter and Latin America," in *Eagle Entangled*, Kenneth Nye, Donald Rothchild, and Robert Lieber, eds. (New York: Longmans, Green, 1979), p. 291.

3. Interview with David Newson, October 27, 1982.

4. This point has been treated by Dimitri Simes, "The New Soviet Challenge," *Foreign Policy*, no. 56 (Fall 1984): 113–31, and by John M. Joyce, "The Old Russian Legacy," *Foreign Policy* 55 (Summer 1984): 132–53.

5. Vance, *Hard Choices*, p. 441.

6. Ibid.

7. William J. Jorden, the United States ambassador to Panama, provides an account of Vance's role in advancing the negotiations, particularly with the appointment of Linowitz. *Panama Odyssey*, pp. 343–44. See also William J. Lanouette, "The Panama Canal Treaties—Playing in Peoria and in the Senate," *National Journal*, October 8, 1977, pp. 1556–62; Margaret Scranton, "The Panama Canal Treaties and the Politics of Change," unpublished paper given at the International Studies Association meeting, Toronto, 1979. Scranton notes that the treaty texts reflected changes about "enforcing cooperation through military intervention" and ability "to work with, rather than against leftist governments." Opposition to the treaties demonstrated the deeply rooted view that the United States had the right to intervene militarily whenever enough people claimed its interests threatened. It demonstrated the demand for action whenever others seemed to be "pushing us around."

8. Lowenthal, "Jimmy Carter and Latin America," p. 292.

9. Dept. of State *Bulletin*, February 1977, pp. 121–22.

10. Ibid., January 1979, pp. 1–2. Also M. Glen Johnson, "The Development of Human Rights Criteria as a Guide to Foreign Policy-Making in the United States," unpublished paper given at the International Studies Association meeting, Toronto, 1979.

11. 95th Congress, 1st sess., *Foreign Assistance and Related Program Appropriations: Hearings by the Committee on Appropriations* (Washington, D.C.: Government Printing Office, 1977), pp. 161, 194. Carter gave human rights a larger place when he addressed the U.N. General Assembly in March 1977. Dept. of State *Bulletin*, April 11, 1977, pp. 329–33.

12. Cyrus Vance, "Human Rights and Foreign Policy," *Georgia Journal of International and Comparative Law* 7 (1977): 231–87; Dept. of State *Bulletin*, May 23, 1977, pp. 505–6.

13. Dept. of State *Bulletin*, June 1977, p. 70.

14. The resolution passed, 14 to 0, with 8 abstentions (Argentina, Brazil, Colombia, Chile, El Salvador, Guatemala, Paraguay, and Uruguay) and 3 absences.

15. Schoultz, *Human Rights*, p. 118. Howard Warshawsky, "The Institutionalization of Morality in Policy-Making: A Case Study of the Human Rights Bureau," unpublished paper given at the International Studies Association meeting, 1979.

16. Brown, *The Faces of Power*, p. 469.

17. Schoultz, *Human Rights*, p. 118.

18. Carter opposed legislation requiring United States representatives to the Inter-American and African Development Banks to vote against loans or technical assistance to human rights violators and to extend this rule to loans by the World Bank. Efforts continued throughout 1977 to make the international lending institutions conform. Senator Robert Dole and Representative Clarence Long, the latter chairman of the foreign operations subcommittee of the House Appropriations Committee, favored legislation withholding financing to whatever extent the international banks voted aid to human rights violators. Carter headed off this threat by promising Long he would instruct the U.S. Executive Directors in the Banks to "oppose and vote against" loans to seven gross violators. Thomas M. Franck and Edward Weisband, *Congress, the Presidency and American Foreign Policy* (New York: Oxford University Press, 1979), pp. 92–93.

19. Critics pointed to the administration's failure to sign the optional protocol to the 1966 political convenant that gave individuals the right to petition an international forum or court concerning violators of human rights. There were "certainly as many critics of the Carter Administration for not going further or backsliding as there were anti-human rights critics." Richard B. Lillich, ed., *U.S. Ratification of Human Rights Treaties* (Charlottesville: University of Virginia Press, 1981). Even those who pointed to the gap between rhetoric and accomplishment acknowledged that "the rhetoric and considerable reality of the Carter Administration has given to human rights a saliency in American foreign policy and world politics." David P. Forsythe, "American Foreign Policy and Human Rights: Rhetoric and Reality," *Universal Human Rights*, no. 3 (July–September 1980): 48.

20. Quoted in Schoultz, *Human Rights*, p. 127. On the difficulty of convincing critics that support for human rights is not incompatible with national security see William A. Hazleton, "National Security Interests and Human Rights: A No-Win Situation for the Carter Administration," unpublished paper given at the Midwest Political Science Association meeting, Chicago, 1980. For a convincing argument that the diplomatic and security costs of human rights were surprisingly—and the gains commensurately—significant, see Richard E. Feinberg, "U.S. Human Rights Policy: Latin America," *International Policy Report* 6, no. 1 (October 1980). It grounded American prestige and influence in the hemisphere not upon fear of our military and covert powers, but upon our idealism, and "reestablished the legitimacy of our leadership." Ibid., p. 2.

21. On departing for Moscow in July 1978, Vance referred publicly to the treatment of Anatoly Shcharansky. For an analysis of the Carter administration's application of human rights to the Soviet Union see Roger Hamburg, "The Carter Administration, Human Rights and the Soviet Union," unpublished paper given at the International Studies Association meeting, Washington, 1978. Carter's attempt to argue that verbal emphasis upon human rights was not interference in Soviet internal affairs met virulent reaction. Nevertheless there was an easing of repression against dissidents and more Jews were allowed to emigrate than before.

22. Brzezinski states that he secured Arthur Goldberg to head the American delegation because he would have a major effect. "I was not disappointed. His leadership gave the United States the visibility and impact we desired." *Power and Principle*, p. 300.

23. David P. Forsythe, "American Foreign Policy and Human Rights: Rhetoric and Reality," *Universal Human Rights* 2, no. 3 (July–September 1980): 45.

24. Michael Brenner, *Nuclear Power and Non-Proliferation* (Cambridge: Harvard University Press, 1982), p. 127.

25. Ibid., p. 132.

## Chapter Nine

1. David P. Calleo, *The Imperious Economy* (Cambridge: Harvard University Press, 1982), chs. 6, 7.

2. David N. Schwartz, *NATO's Nuclear Dilemmas* (Washington, D.C.: The Brookings Institution, 1982), p. 212.

3. Ibid., p. 211.

4. Ibid. Vance suggests that British and German concern about how to resolve details of cruise missiles remained. *Hard Choices*, p. 67.

5. Wolfram Hanrieder, *Helmut Schmidt: Perspectives in Politics* (Boulder, Colo.: Westview Press, 1982), p. 26.

6. Schwartz, *NATO's Nuclear Dilemmas*, p. 207.

7. Ibid., p. 208.

8. Ibid.

9. Vance, *Hard Choices*, p. 94.

10. Interview with Robert Hunter.

11. Vance, *Hard Choices*, p. 94.

12. Ibid., p. 95.

13. Ibid.

14. Ibid., pp. 128–29.

15. Ibid., p. 130.

16. Schwartz, *NATO's Nuclear Dilemmas*, p. 244.

17. Brzezinski, *Power and Principle*, p. 308.

18. Schwartz, *NATO's Nuclear Dilemmas*, p. 239.

19. Ibid., pp. 239–40.

## Chapter Ten

1. Cyrus Vance, "The United States and Africa: Building Positive Relationships," Dept. of State *Bulletin*, August 8, 1977, p. 170. Undersecretary Habib was more outspoken in declaring that "only where progress toward social, racial, and political justice has been frustrated has the United States any cause for concern that conditions may arise that are inhospitable to our basic national interests." Dept. of State *Bulletin*, April 4, 1977, p. 319.

2. Ambassador Young explained to a congressional subcommittee that "anything South Africa does must be done because it is in their own national interest. . . . If there is the kind of escalation that is inevitable if majority rule in Rhodesia does not come quickly, then South Africa is also endangered." Dept. of State *Bulletin*, March 21, 1977, pp. 271–72.

3. Michael Clough, *Changing Realities in Southern Africa* (Berkeley: University of California Press, 1982), p. 57; Camelo Mesa-Lago and June S. Belkins, eds., *Cuba in Africa* (Pittsburgh: University of Pittsburgh Press, 1982); Ronald T. Libby, *Toward an Africanized U.S. Policy for Southern Africa* (Berkeley, Calif.: Institute of International Studies, 1980).

4. Ibid., pp. 57–58.

5. Ibid., pp. 88–89.

6. Ibid., pp. 86–87.

7. Brzezinski, *Power and Principle*, pp. 140–41.

8. "Senate Votes to Lift Economic Sanctions against Rhodesia," *Congressional Quarterly, Weekly Report* 37, no. 24 (June 16, 1979): 1185, 1200.

9. Michael Clough, *Changing Realities in Southern Africa*, pp. 44–45.

10. John Newhouse, "Profiles: A Sense of Duty." *New Yorker*, February 14, 1983, pp. 69–74. Newhouse quotes Lord Carrington: "You couldn't leave things as they were . . . the recognition of the Bishop's regime would have led to the most appalling problems—not least the isolation of Britain . . . And it would have intensified the war in Rhodesia. There would have been much more bloodshed . . . and it would have brought the involvement of the Soviet Union. Steady and consistent American support was granted though often without enthusiasm." Ibid., p. 74. This was because some advisers were skeptical of the Thatcher Government's commitment, but this was not true of Vance.

11. Cyrus Vance, *Hard Choices*, p. 266.

12. Ibid., p. 275.

13. Ronald T. Libby, *Toward an Africanized U.S Policy for Southern Africa*, pp. 100–103. See also Thomas Callaghy, *South Africa in Southern Africa* (New York: Praeger, 1983).

## Chapter Eleven

1. Jeffrey Z. Rubin, *Dynamics of Third Party Intervention: Kissinger in the Middle East* (New York: Praeger, 1981), pp. 109–10, 129–30, 160–64, 260–80. Kissinger's step-by-step diplomacy despite successes was limited to marginal issues "calculated to protect and enhance the image of Henry Kissinger . . . One cannot understand the behavior of Kissinger, the mediator, without also taking account of Kissinger's tremendous ego and his perception of himself as indispensable." Ibid., p. 132. Rubin confirms Quandt's assessment that Kissinger could not resist being Machiavellian by holding back concessions made by one side so as to appear to have won more than either could have expected. See also Ishaq I. Chanayem and Alden H. Voth, *American Middle East Policy* (New York: Praeger, 1984), pp. 173–75.

2. Interview with William Quandt, September 19, 1983.

3. Carter, *Keeping the Faith*, pp. 350–55.

4. Silver, *Begin*, pp. 194–95.

5. The single negotiating-text strategy by Carter and Vance at Camp David had important advantages over seeking concessions from both sides. It made extreme positions irrelevant and required each party to make only one decision at the end. Jeffrey A. Rubin, *Dynamics of Third Party Intervention*, p. 109.

6. "Thus a decision was made, no doubt largely at the behest of Carter, to focus the discussions primarily on the fate of the Sinai desert . . . as well as the establishment of normal diplomatic and economic relations between Israel and Egypt. The much more intractable and enduring issues in the Middle East—the fate of the West Bank, Palestinian autonomy, and the fate of Jerusalem—appear to have . . . sidetracked . . ." Ibid., pp. 29–30.

7. Brzezinski, *Power and Principle*, p. 265.

8. Ibid., pp. 103–4.

9. Vance, *Hard Choices*, pp. 103–4.

10. Ibid., p. 229.

11. The most incisive account of Begin's double-dealing is in Mark Heller, "Begin's False Autonomy," *Foreign Policy* 37 (Winter 1979–80): 111–32. Although it was in Israel's long-run interest to find some form of autonomy or independence for the West Bank, Begin's commitment to autonomy never went beyond lip service, and Palestinians on the West Bank had every right to be suspicious of provisions in

the treaty "intended to legitimate the continued occupation, and perhaps even the eventual annexation, of the West Bank and Gaza by Israel." Pp. 113–14.

12. Vance, *Hard Choices*, p. 225.

13. Silver, *Begin*, pp. 200–201.

14. Vance, *Hard Choices*, p. 236.

15. Ibid., p. 241.

16. Ibid.

17. Ibid., p. 243.

18. Ibid., p. 245.

19. Interview with Harold Saunders, December 21, 1983.

20. Vance, *Hard Choices*, p. 249.

21. Ibid., pp. 253–54.

22. Ibid.

## Chapter Twelve

1. William D. Jackson, "Policy Assessment at the Crossroads: The Soviets and SALT," *Bulletin of the Atomic Scientists* 5, no. 4 (April 1979): 10–14.

2. Talbott, *Endgame*, p. 148.

3. Ibid., pp. 138–42.

4. Ibid., p. 140. Rowny had been on the negotiation team since 1973, and Harold Brown had "renewed Rowny's appointment at the outset of the Carter Administration, largely because the Administration had hopes of winning Jackson's backing for SALT II. Many on the delegation were now worried that Rowny would stay on until the treaty was concluded, accumulating ammunition, then resign in protest and join the Jackson-Nitze forces, who were expected to oppose ratification." Ibid. This is exactly what happened.

5. Ibid., pp. 147–48.

6. Ibid.

7. Brzezinski, *Power and Principle*, pp. 147–48; Vance, *Hard Choices*, pp. 101–4.

8. Brzezinski, *Power and Principle*, p. 188; also pp. 319–23.

9. Interview with *New York Times* reporter Bernard Gwertzman, Washington, D.C., September 20, 1983. Gwertzman argued that Vance let down the public side of his job and thereby handicapped himself. "A secretary of state is only perceived to be as strong on the inside as he is on the outside." Given the way the Washington press corps operated, Vance did not seem strong, especially since Brzezinski not only had propinquity, but was closer to Carter in style.

10. "National Security Policy Integration," paper for President's Reorganization Project, September 1979. See also Duncan Clarke, "The Odeen Report: Findings and Recommendations," in *Decision-Making for Arms Limitation*, Hans G. Brauch and Duncan Clarke, eds. (Cambridge, Mass.: Ballinger, 1983), pp. 6–15. "Brzezinski's staff was faulted for its managerial deficiencies: too many meetings of the NSC's two senior committees, the Special Coordinating Committee (SCC) and the Policy Review Committee (PRC); meetings often lacked a clear purpose; preparatory papers for these meetings were usually produced by one department with little coordination with the others; and the quality of NSC and OMB [Office of Management and Budget] analysis was 'uneven.' Also, materials presented for the president's review often did not facilitate his decision-making. Finally, the NSC staff was

criticized for not clearly communicating presidential decisions and their rationale to the bureaucracy and, then, overseeing their implementation." Ibid. It was also faulted for inadequate procedures for interagency crisis planning, a recommendation that was never carried out.

11. Vance, *Hard Choices*, p. 101.

12. Ibid., p. 102.

13. The speech was largely Carter's and "contained much to my surprise a great number of extremely toughly worded statements." Brzezinski, *Power and Principle*, p. 320. The foreign policy adviser had expected Vance to object, and when the Secretary of State remained silent, Brzezinski let the statements stand. But here was a strange admission. Of course Brzezinski could not have objected to the anti-Soviet tone of the President's speech.

14. Quoted in Vance, *Hard Choices*, p. 76.

15. Ibid., pp. 76–77.

16. Brzezinski, *Power and Principle*, p. 189.

17. Vance tried to counter this point by suggesting that Mondale go.

18. Brzezinski, *Power and Principle*, p. 207.

19. Ibid., p. 217. Upon his return, Brzezinski stopped in Tokyo and "on my own initiative" when briefing Prime Minister Fukuda urged that both he and the Japanese foreign minister go ahead with the Chinese-Japanese friendship treaty including the anti-hegemony clause. The latter was Beijing's anti-Soviet formula.

20. Quoted in ibid., p. 220.

21. Ibid., p. 221.

22. Talbott, *Endgame*, p. 159.

23. The Carter administration's handling of China recognition in relation to Congress is in "Executive-Legislative Consultation on China Policy, 1978–79," released by the Committee on Foreign Affairs, June 1980.

24. Michel Oksenberg, "Sino-American Relations," *Foreign Affairs* 61 (1982–83): 188.

25. Brzezinski, *Power and Principle*, p. 230.

26. Ibid., p. 231.

27. Ibid., p. 232. This passage appears in quotation marks and probably is in Brzezinski's diary.

28. Vance, *Hard Choices*, p. 112.

29. Carter, *Keeping Faith*, p. 234.

30. Brzezinski, *Power and Principle*, p. 459.

31. Ibid., p. 458.

## Chapter Thirteen

1. Vance, *Hard Choices*, p. 317.

2. Brzezinski, *Power and Principle*, p. 360.

3. James E. Carter, "Fall of the Shah," *Time Magazine*, October 18, 1982, p. 49.

4. Gary Sick, the NSC staff member concerned with Iran, wrote of Nixon-Kissinger policy: " 'Blank checks' is not too strong an expression to describe the deal for it was spelled out in a subsequent memorandum to the government that 'we would not second guess the Shah, that he would define his own needs for military equipment and we would not impose our views.' " "Washington's Encounter with the Iranian Revolution," in *The Iranian Revolution and the Islamic Republic* (Washington, D.C.: Woodrow Wilson Center, 1982).

5. Vance, *Hard Choices*, p. 319.

6. Figures from *U.S. Military Sales to Iran* (Washington, D.C.: Government Printing Office, 1981), p. vii; *Congressional Quarterly, Weekly Report* 38, no. 1 (January 1980): 7.

7. Sick, "Washington's Encounter with the Iranian Revolution," p. 128.

8. Statement by Secretary Vance, opening session of the CENTO Council of Ministers, Dept. of State *Bulletin*, June 1978, pp. 24–26.

9. Vance, *Hard Choices*, p. 324.

10. Ibid, pp. 325–26.

11. William Sullivan, *Mission to Iran* (New York: Norton, 1981), pp. 156–57.

12. Brzezinski, *Power and Principle*, p. 364.

13. Ibid.

14. Ibid.

15. Brzezinski argues that Vance resisted providing the Iranian military with crowd control devices because the British were supplying them.

16. Ibid., pp. 367–68.

17. Ibid., p. 375. "This message represented the clearest and most direct effort to get the Shah to do what needed to be done without the United States assuming, in effect, the responsibility of governing Iran on his behalf."

18. Ibid., p. 376.

19. Ibid., p. 380.

20. For the Kerensky analogy, interview with David Aaron, New York, October 10, 1983.

21. Brzezinski, *Power and Principle*, p. 396. Brzezinski's explanation for the failure reveals, more than anything else, the shallowness of his sense of history. Ibid., pp. 395–97.

22. Two-thirds of the respondents in a *New York Times*/CBS poll supported Carter's policy of not taking sides during the Iranian upheaval. *New York Times*, March 2, 1979.

23. Richard Feinberg, "The Recent Rapid Redefinition of U.S. Interests and Diplomacy in Central America," in *Central America: International Dimension of the Crisis*, Richard Feinberg, ed. (London and New York: Holmes and Meier, 1982), p. 66. See also Bernard Diederich, *Somoza and the Legacy of U.S. Involvement in Central America* (New York: Dutton, 1981); and Anastasio Somoza, *Nicaragua Betrayed* (Boston: Western Islands Press, 1980).

24. Communication from Ambassador Vaky, July 13, 1984.

25. Feinberg, "The Recent Rapid Redefinition," p. 67.

26. Ibid., p. 66.

27. Robert Pastor reports that, of the centrist leaders to whom he spoke, none who went over to the Sandinistas, and who were ultimately forced out by them, has ever said that under the circumstances he would have acted otherwise. Interview, College Park, Maryland, December 19, 1983.

28. On May 20, 1979, President Lopez Portillo announced that Mexico was breaking relations with Nicaragua because of what he called a record of "horrendous genocide" by the Somoza government. *New York Times*, May 21, 1979.

29. Ibid., June 24, 1979.

30. *New York Times*, August 17, 1979. "Central America at the Crossroads," testimony of Viron P. Vaky before the subcommittee on inter-American affairs of the House of Representatives, 96th Congress, 1st sess., September 11 and 12, 1979.

31. Orrin G. Hatch, *New York Times*, August 1, 1979.

## Chapter Fourteen

1. Norman Podhoretz, "The Carter Stalemate," *New York Times*, July 9, 1978; the same author's "The Red Menace," ibid., May 14, 1978; "Countering Soviet Imperialism," ibid., May 31; "The Cold War Again?", ibid., June 11.

2. *The Gallup Poll: Public Opinion, 1979* (Wilmington, Del.: Scholarly Resources Press, 1980), p. 123. Opponents argued that Russia could not be trusted and that a false sense of security from such a treaty would increase the likelihood of war.

3. Dimitri Simes, "The Anti-Soviet Brigade," *Foreign Policy* 37 (Winter 1979–80): 30.

4. Paul H. Nitze, "Is SALT II a Fair Deal for the United States," in *Where We Stand on SALT* (Washington, D.C.: Committee on the Present Danger, 1977). See also Nitze, "Assuring Strategic Stability in an Era of Detente," *Foreign Affairs* 54, no. 2 (January 1976): 207–32.

5. The Soviets had backed away from confrontation over the mining of Haiphong harbor and in the Middle East war of 1973. Bjorkman and Zamostny, cite a plethora of articles in *Pravda and Izvestiya* as well as official statements rejecting the balance of terror as the best means of maintaining peace. "Soviet Politics and Strategy," *World Politics* 36, no. 2 (January 1984): 204.

6. Warner Schilling, "U.S. Strategic Nuclear Concepts in the 1970s: The Search for Sufficiently Equivalent Countervailing Parity," *International Security* 6, no. 2 (Fall 1981): 69.

7. Aaron L. Friedberg, "What SALT Can (and Cannot) Do," *Foreign Policy* 57 (Winter 1978–79): 100.

8. For detailed analysis see Dimitri Simes, "The Anti-Soviet Brigade"; also Jerry W. Sanders, *Peddlers of Crisis: The Committee on the Present Danger and the Politics of Containment* (Boston: South End Press, 1983).

9. As Bernard Gwertzman put it, the media and especially the Washington press corps was the fourth branch of government and many of its Washington "legislators" had already rendered an opinion on the Carter administration that doomed SALT. Interview September 20, 1983.

10. Pat Towell, "To Win on SALT II, Carter Must Overcome Ideological Standoff Lasting a Decade," *Congressional Quarterly, Weekly Report* 37, no. 24 (June 1979): 1177–81.

11. *New York Times*, February 4, 1979.

12. Ibid., March 9. The hawks and doves were both now in opposition.

13. Ibid., April 8.

14. For Carter's speech and the SALT treaties see *Congressional Quarterly, Weekly Report* 37, no. 25 (June 1979): 1221–40.

15. Vance's testimony is in *Congressional Quarterly, Weekly Report* 37, no. 28 (July 1979): 1383–86.

16. *New York Times*, July 11, 1979. Also testimony before the Senate Armed Services Committee, ibid., July 30.

17. Vance testimony in ibid., July 11.

18. See Christopher Makins, "Bringing in the Allies," *Foreign Policy* 35 (Summer 1979): 91–108.

19. Testimony by Nitze and Rowny in *Congressional Quarterly, Weekly Report* 37, no. 28 (July 1979): 1385–86.

20. *New York Times*, July 15, 1979.

21. Interview with Harold Brown, Washington, December 8, 1983.

22. Testimony by Kissinger in *Congressional Quarterly, Weekly Report* 37, no.

31 (July 14, 1979): 1396–98; *New York Times,* August 1, 1979. Alexander Haig testimony against the treaty in ibid., August 5.

23. Simes, "The Anti-Soviet Brigade," pp. 34–35.

24. Freeman Dyson, "Reflections: Weapons and Hope," *New Yorker,* February 20, 1984, p. 83.

25. Gloria Duffy, "Crisis Prevention in Cuba," in Alexander L. George, ed., *Managing U.S.-Soviet Rivalry* (Boulder, Colo.: Westview Press, 1983).

26. Commenting on Church's reaction a few days later, Georgi Arbatov observed: "There is nothing as dangerous as a scared dove."

27. Gloria Duffy, "Crisis Prevention in Cuba," pp. 307–8.

28. Vance, *Hard Choices,* p. 394. "The tension between visceral anti-Sovietism and an attempt to regulate dangerous competition could no longer be maintained. The scales tipped toward those favoring confrontation." Loc. cit.

29. On January 3 the President asked the Senate to defer consideration of the treaty. At the same time he announced that the U.S. would take no action contrary to the terms of the treaty so long as the Soviets did the same. "This prevented the unraveling of restraints on the strategic competition at a time of high tension." Ibid., p. 389.

## Chapter Fifteen

1. Hamilton Jordan, *Crisis: The Last Year of the Carter Presidency* (New York: Putnam, 1982), p. 29.

2. Ibid.

3. Ibid.

4. Ibid., p. 30. Also Terence Smith, "Why Carter Admitted the Shah," in *America in Captivity: Points of Decision in the Hostage Crisis,* special issue of *New Yorker,* 1981, pp. 42–47.

5. John Felton, "Carter Calls for Restraint in Reacting to Takeover of U.S. Embassy in Iran," *Congressional Quarterly, Weekly Report* 37, no. 45 (1979): 2569–70.

6. Terence Smith, "Why Carter Admitted the Shah," p. 47; Carter, *Keeping Faith,* pp. 454–55; Jordan, *Crisis,* p. 31.

7. Ibid.

8. Brzezinski encountered Bazargan and Yazdi at a conference in late October in Algeria, and when they expressed skepticism that the Shah could be seeking asylum for purely medical reasons Brzezinski told them such a discussion was humiliating. His point of view remained consistent—we should not let a third-rate nation dictate what we did about the Shah, only considerations of honor and integrity and never of pride and concern seem to have occurred to him. *Power and Principle,* p. 476.

9. Ibid., pp. 480–81.

10. Vance, *Hard Choices,* p. 377.

11. Brzezinski, *Power and Principle,* p. 481.

12. Interview with Vance, in Thomas Hammond, *Red Flag over Afghanistan* (Boulder, Colo.: Westview Press, 1983), p. 115. Muhammad Azmi, "Soviet Politico—Military Penetration in Afghanistan," unpublished paper, 1984, Miami University.

13. Hammond, *Red Flag,* p. 115.

14. Ibid.

15. Ibid.

16. Vance, *Hard Choices,* p. 386.

17. Interview with Brzezinski in Hammond, *Red Flag over Afghanistan*, p. 63. Former ambassador Robert Neumann tried to change this approach; the current ambassador, Theodore Eliot, urged restraint. Ibid., pp. 62–63.

18. *Washington Post*, October 17, 1980, cited in ibid., p. 135. Henry S. Bradsher, *Afghanistan and the Soviet Union* (Durham, N.C.: Duke University Press, 1983) argues that the dominant Soviet explanation became the need to defend Soviet security interests, p. 155.

19. Ibid., p. 110. Based on a telephone interview with Vance by Hammond, January 6, 1982. Information about American protests was later supplied by Marshall Shulman who in a letter to Congressman Lee Hamilton listed four other meetings with the Soviets prior to the invasion, December 8, 11, 15, and 17. Ibid., pp. 110–11. For Shulman testimony see *New York Times*, January 31, 1980.

20. Vance, *Hard Choices*, p. 387. Henry Bradsher, in his authoritative study *Afghanistan and the Soviet Union*, states that Soviet delay in not invading much earlier "argues strongly for a defensive motive" behind the Soviet action and not part of a Soviet grand strategy of expansionism, pp. 159–60.

21. *New York Times*, January 16, 1980.

22. Carter's characterization of his reaction seemed exaggerated. "My impression of the Russians has changed [more] drastically in the last week than even the previous two and a half years before that . . . This action . . . has made a more dramatic change in my own opinion of what the Soviets' ultimate goals are than anything they've done." He stated that the Soviet invasion posed "the most serious threat to world peace since the Second World War." But Soviet intervention was neither unexpected nor did it represent a departure from general policy. "Though important, the intervention was not all that cataclysmic; it is not self-evident that it should have had such an upsetting effect on the President's views." Thomas Hart, "Perceiving Afghanistan," in *Cognitive Dynamics and International Politics* ed. C. Johnson (London: Francis Pinter, 1982), pp. 178–86.

23. *New York Times*, January 24, 1980.

24. Brzezinski, *Power and Principle*, p. 460.

25. Ibid., p. 462.

26. Schmidt interview, *New York Times*, January 10, 1980.

27. Brzezinski, *Power and Principle*, p. 485.

28. Ibid., p. 492.

29. Ibid., p. 494.

30. Ibid., p. 499. NSC and State Department interviewers alike spoke of Brzezinski's near obsession with military force. He had in mind the example of Kerensky according to Aaron; unless moderates were ruthless they would give way to doctrinaires.

31. Interview with Harold Saunders, Washington, D.C., December 21, 1983.

## Chapter Sixteen

1. I.M. Destler, Leslie H. Gelb and Anthony Lake, *Our Own Worst Enemy*, pp. 216–19.

2. Thomas L. Hughes, "Carter and the Management of Contradictions," *Foreign Policy* 31 (1978): 34–35.

3. Even academics sympathetic to the administration's foreign policy approach were not averse to measuring it against some mythical consistency and asking

perfection, while taking little if any account of the powerful reversal of public and congressional support for détente.

4. David P. Calleo, *The Imperious Economy* (Cambridge: Harvard University Press, 1982), p. 143.

5. Ibid. By November the dollar's rapid depreciation led to a much publicized "rescue package" of domestic monetary measures and foreign credits.

6. Interview with David Newsom, October 27, 1982.

# Bibliographical Essay

A biography of Vance as Secretary of State became possible with publication of two memoirs—his own, *Hard Choices,* and that of Zbigniew Brzezinski, *Power and Principle.* Vance received assistance from Eric Newsom, a foreign service officer who spent months interpreting the mountains of State Department material that will only become available to the historian perhaps twenty or thirty years from now. *Power and Principle* derives much of its authority from the inclusion of long and pointed diary excerpts; it is marvelously revealing of its author's positions and recommendations as well as those of the President, Secretary of State, and others.

*Keeping Faith* by President Carter, *Crisis* by Hamilton Jordan, and Ambassador William Sullivan's account of the Shah's last months, *Mission to Iran,* all provide more information. Members of Brzezinski's staff have published accounts in scholarly journals.

I have especially benefitted from *Endgame,* Strobe Talbott's inside discussion of SALT II, and from Jerel Rosati's dissertation at American University, "The Impact of Beliefs on Behavior: The Foreign Policy of the Carter Administration," a shortened version of which appears in *Foreign Policy Decision Making.*

The following individuals granted interviews that were very helpful:

From the *State Department:* Cyrus Vance, Warren Christopher, David Newsom, Paul C. Warnke, Anthony Lake, Arnold Raphael, Harold Saunders, Charles William Mayne, Richard Holbrooke, Marshall Shulman, Eric Newsom, and Viron Vaky. The *NSC Staff:* David Aaron, Samuel Huntington, Robert Hunter, William Quandt, and Robert Pastor. From the *Department of Defense:* Harold Brown. *Vance's associates from the Johnson administration:*

Robert McNamara, Townsend Hoopes, and McGeorge Bundy. Also newsmen Bernard Gwertzman and Leslie Gelb *(New York Times)*, and Strobe Talbott *(Time Magazine)*.

Two sets of interviews with Vance were highly informative—one in the Lyndon B. Johnson Library in Austin, the other in the U.S. Army War College in Carlisle Barracks, Pennsylvania.

The reader may easily find my other sources, whether articles or books, in the notes to the present volume.

# Index